Only Get Better?

A guide to social services
performance measurement processes
for front line staff

David Burnham

Russell House Publishing

Russell House Publishing
First published in 2006 by:
Russell House Publishing Ltd.
4 St. George's House
Uplyme Road
Lyme Regis
Dorset DT7 3LS
Tel: 01297-443948
Fax: 01297-442722
e-mail: help@russellhouse.co.uk
www.russellhouse.co.uk

British Library Cataloguing-in-publication Data:

ISBN: 1-903855-91-8; 978-1-903855-91-1

Typeset by TW Typesetting, Plymouth, Devon
Printed by Alden Press, Oxford

About Russell House Publishing

RHP is a group of social work, probation, education and youth and
community work practitioners and academics working in
collaboration with a professional publishing team.
Our aim is to work closely with the field to produce innovative
and valuable materials to help managers, trainers, practitioners
and students.
We are keen to receive feedback on publications and new ideas for
future projects.
For details of our other publications please visit our website or ask
us for a catalogue. Contact details are on this page.

Contents

To Milo's favourite walking companion

Acknowledgements

Hundreds of people have contributed to the thinking that developed into this book, both unwittingly and with more focussed comments. I have to thank the many staff in Lancashire Social Services and beyond who have had to put up with odd questions and silly exercises at my hands for a number of years. I also have to thank Lancashire County Council for the encouragement to complete this project. But I owe a special debt to the people mentioned below, for a range of reasons. So thank you to Linda Drury, David Rogers, Jane Williams, Ian Phillips, Sophie Tucker, Tony Hubbard, Nick Miller, Sue Dean, Donna Talbot, John Mercer, Steve Purdy, Peter Francis, Michael Murphy, Richard Jones, Blair McPherson, Joanne Platt, Kim Haworth, Pat Damms, Liz Holden, Liz Drury, Alice Burnham, Milo Dee, Tom Daniels, Mark Fletcher, Helen Robinson, Dot Metcalf, Alan Bunting, David Henderson and Jenny Phillips.

About the Author

David Burnham works as Head of Information for Lancashire Adult Social Services – although previously his role included responsibility for information and performance for children's services too. He has considerable experience as an operational manager, trainer and in social care education. He is currently an ADSS representative on the Performance Co-ordinating Group. He has had a number of articles on social care published, most recently on respite vouchers (*Community Care*, February 2001) performance management (*Community Care*, February 2004) and IT in social care (*British Journal of Health Computing*, November 2005).

The book sums up succinctly the system I am part of and abhor.
It also gives me hope for the future by showing the way it could be changed to enable me and lots of others to gain live feedback from the people we are trying to help.
This in turn could have the beneficial effect of making social workers proud again about being part of a worthwhile profession which does a good honest job of work.

John Mercer, Team Manager (mental health of older people)

Introduction

Bewilderment and distrust

Performance targets are everywhere. Production targets in industry and sales targets in retail have been joined over the last decade by a huge range of government performance targets in the public sector. The response of front line social services staff to this relatively new and still evolving performance regime has been similar to other public servants. There is cautious acceptance in some places, while in others there is bewilderment and distrust. But many social services staff dismiss performance indicators and all they represent as irrelevant, misleading or oppressive.

Inspectorates are everywhere across public service too. Using performance information and other material, inspectorates make judgements about the quality and overall performance of public services; schools, hospitals, prisons, and children's and adult's social care services. In the main, senior managers in social services accept the performance assessment regimes and work closely with the various inspectorates.

This acceptance by senior managers of the performance regime and the distrust of the same processes by front line staff provides a challenge for all councils with social services responsibilities (CSSRs). The conflict implied in these differences in perception has in some places fostered resentment, subversion and bullying; none of which contributes to the quality of services offered to vulnerable people.

Engaging the front line

Audit Commission documents often use the phrase 'The Golden Thread' when discussing performance measurement disciplines in local government. This describes the strand of meaning and influence that, it is claimed, should connect the objectives of council cabinet members right through to the individual goals identified in annual appraisals of each front line worker. Most guidance about these processes is directed at managers – senior managers at that. If any sort of thread, cotton even, is to form the connection throughout the organisation, then serious attention has to be paid to the other end of the skein – the front line. Front line staff often feel left out of the debate about performance measurement, even though they are the people who contribute most to the service outcome. This book offers a guide to performance measurement and assessment processes used by the

Commission for Social Care Inspection (CSCI) to make judgements about how well adult and older people's social services and children's social services in local councils are 'performing'. Although the meaning and technicalities of the Performance Indicators (PI) and other judgement processes are described here, the major purpose of the book is to offer a guide to front line staff and team managers about what the principles behind these processes are, how these affect them, how they can establish a role in the process and how they can use the performance assessment cycle to the advantage of the people they serve. The book may also be useful for **students, academics, social work teachers, service users, user group representatives** and **voluntary agencies**.

Measurement, assessment and management

The phrase 'performance measurement and assessment' is used here to describe the complex set of processes which are operated by the CSCI for specific reasons. Although much of what is described and discussed here is often, in local government circles, referred to as 'performance management' the use of that phrase is, in my view, inaccurate. There are two general uses of the phrase 'performance management'. First of all in discussions about human resource management the phrase is used to describe the attention paid to the work of individual staff to help them improve their individual 'performance'. The broader use of the phrase 'performance management' refers to everything an organisation does to improve its overall performance. This implies a comprehensive set of disciplines, which the CSCI may encourage CSSRs to aspire to, but which implies a much more complete organisational response than the performance assessment cycle currently involves. In social care we may aspire to performance management but few CSSRs do it, so I use the more accurate 'performance measurement' for what CSSRs do and 'performance assessment' for what the CSCI does. See the beginning of Chapter 3 for a longer debate on this.

England, Scotland, Wales, Northern Ireland and partner agencies

I have already used the ugly acronym CSSR. I use this to refer to all 150 English councils with social services responsibilities because it is generally used by government departments and agencies. The phrase also encompasses social care services for both adults and children – at a time when structural arrangements for social services for adults and children are changing as a result of the requirements of the Children Act 2004. While the detail discussed here is English, the history and principles discussed in Chapter 2 and the analysis and proposals in Chapters 4 and 5 are as relevant for the rest of Britain and in other English public services as they are for English CSSRs. Detailed arrangements in Scotland, Wales and Northern Ireland differ considerably from England and from each other. A brief appendix refers to performance arrangements in the other three nations of Britain and to other English public services.

Broad principles

Currently there is little literature about performance measurement and assessment directed at a social care audience. This might be because the disciplines are so new, or it may be because the procedures don't sit still long enough for them to be accurately explained. The main danger in writing a book about processes which change on an annual basis and whose subject matter is bound up with political priorities, is that the detail will be out of date before the print is dry. The definitions of the national PIs are subject to annual review when new indicators are added and others deleted. What's more measurement and assessment methodology is developing all the time. The response of councils and the Association of Directors of Social Services (ADSS) to the process is becoming more sophisticated; and the bigger picture of how the performance of councils as a whole is judged is developing too. So the subject is a moving target. In order to mitigate the ephemeral nature of some of the content I have tried to be clear which aspects of the process are subject to frequent review and which are likely to have a longer shelf life. But the overall task is to pin down the broad principles behind the current process in order to widen the increasingly strident debate about performance.

Keeping it up to date

You will notice that a lot of the references in this book are web addresses, many of them belonging to government agencies. If you are tempted to believe anything factual in the book (the opinions are of course my own alone) please check those web sites before committing yourself to anything drastic.

There are some technical aspects to this subject and some of the language used might not be immediately familiar. I have included a glossary of terms at the end to help those new to performance measurement and assessment and I have tried to be clear in describing the detail about how the process works. As a result some of the explanations may appear simple to those accustomed to these ideas: conversely, I apologise if any explanations are still baffling.

The structure of the book

- The first chapter outlines the pressure many social workers experience as a result of the current performance regime.
- Chapter 2 contains an explanation of the principles underpinning the performance measurement and assessment regime and the development of specific aspects of it over the last couple of decades.
- The third chapter looks in detail at the current processes, how PIs are supposed to work, the process of making an overall judgement and several of the problems associated with PIs.
- Chapter 4 offers an analysis of the process: the theoretical basis, the outcomes for the various stakeholders and its consequences (deliberate and unintended).
- The final chapter includes a set of ideas for first line managers and front line staff to help them live with the current performance regime. It also offers several ideas for how the processes could be improved.

Each chapter has a brief summary at the end and also includes one or two exercises. These are included as an opportunity for teams and groups of staff and students to develop their own responses to the ideas.

Chapter 1

Setting the Scene

Embraced with open arms

All of us try to improve how we perform in so many aspects of our lives. As children we try at school to get better at reading or spelling, to win the approval of our teachers and parents. We try to show how good we are in order to get picked – for a job, for a place at college, for a team. At work we strive to do the best we can for the people we are working for or to gain the respect of others. We spend hours learning a musical instrument, initially because we are told to, and then because it gives immense pleasure, or might become a career. And of course we also try (whether we are proud of it or not) to improve how we do some activities to be better than the other person.

So it's a common human trait to want to improve our performance. There are several characteristics that need to be in place to ensure you are successful in attempting to enhance your performance for a given activity. You have to:

- Care about it. The activity has to have **meaning** for you.
- See that things could be made better – or put another way, you have to have the **capacity to see what's wrong** or undeveloped.
- Have the **imagination or intellect** to see how it could be made better.
- **Believe** that performance can be improved.
- Have the **power to improve things**. It has to be up to you.
- Have or know how to gain the **ability to improve performance**.
- Have the **resource and support to invest** in enhancing your performance.
- Know when things have improved and how. You need a **goal**.

There is no deep insight here. This is simply a list I have developed in introducing front line workers to performance measurement disciplines. But psychological literature confirms this view, especially the need to have identified goals to improve performance. Locke et al. developed a set of hypotheses about performance improvement, which have been tested in a number of subsequent studies (Locke and Latham, 1990). The key, according to Locke is that task performance is regulated by conscious goals. They see the identification of goals as the central feature predicting real enhancement of any performance. Goals direct attention and effort, enhance persistence, mobilise new learning strategies and provide feedback. Feedback in turn renews attention, strengthens persistence and so on. Locke also suggests that difficult goals result in higher levels of performance than easy goals, as long as commitment and the resources to achieve those goals are present. And specific goals result in better performance than generalised goals. However, goals that are too challenging intimidate people. In this case short term interim goals (often called milestones) are crucial to success. The studies furthermore suggest that performance and performance improvement are also affected by monetary incentives, time limits, knowledge of results, participation in decision making, the degree of commitment and competition.

It is relatively easy to see how these ideas work with individuals seeking to improve their performance in a whole range of situations. However, most of the literature relates to activities of large commercial organisations, not too dissimilar from a social services environment.

It does not take much imagination to see how these ideas can be relevant to social care services. The social worker's task is often to help the family or individual respond positively to difficult circumstances or to learn new coping skills, i.e. to improve their performance. And the way work is done rests upon practices, therapies and operational frameworks which demand explicit goal setting activity, the use of milestones and feedback loops. So the introduction of explicit performance measurement frameworks and disciplines into the social care world should have been embraced with open arms.

In fact, this has been far from the case. In February 2004 a number of social workers in Liverpool City Council went on strike. They had a number of grievances, a major one being that the organisation was 'target driven' rather than led by the needs of the citizens of Liverpool. The Liverpool social workers expressed the opinion that targets were imposed from above and had little meaning for them and the people they worked with. One of the strikers said 'the council's attitude disregards social workers' professional judgement of how best to deal with clients . . . Now work is judged on targets'. Another claimed that 'Managers have leaned on social workers to take kids off the child protection register . . . to get the figures improved, even when the social worker didn't think it appropriate' (Guardian Society, 2004). The response of this group of staff may have been extreme but many front line workers across the country would recognise their grievances.

What was being referred to was the workers' view of the way their managers have interpreted the Performance Assessment Framework (PAF). This is a set of 50 measures of organisational performance or Performance Indicators (PIs) each CSSR has to report on each year. The performance of CSSRs against each of these PIs has, since May 2002, been incorporated (with other qualitative information about the services of the CSSR) into two judgements; one about how well each CSSR is serving people and the other about what its prospects are for improvement. From this an overall judgement is determined, expressed in terms of a star rating. Each Authority has since 2002 been categorised as having up to three stars; three star social service departments being the best and zero star departments seen as 'failing'.

Performance indicators

So why is performance management in social care such a problem? Why so much anger at an attempt by central government to help social services improve their performance? The practice tales below present several of the possible reasons. The experiences of these five social workers demonstrate some of the frustrations with how performance management is experienced on the front line. The names are fictitious but the situations will be familiar to many. All these frustrations are down to the local management of performance measurement.

> **Practice Tale 1.** *Abel is a social worker with a team in a London borough. Mostly he works with Looked After Children and he has a bit of way with adolescent boys who are difficult to place. He is working with Ben, a 13-year-old who has been with a foster family for ten months and appears to have settled well. Abel is relieved about this because the boy had had bad experiences before and was moved a couple of times. So Abel was particularly upset when the foster carers reported that Ben had started running with a set of youths they didn't like. Abel spent a great deal of time over the last month with Ben and the carers working with increasing intensity – dealing with broken promises, suspicions of petty theft in the home and late nights. But now with barely concealed threats to other children in the home Abel knows it's time to break the pattern and move Ben on. But his team manager won't hear of a move. She finally relents after a direct confrontation, but advises Abel not to record the move until the following month. 'Our targets', is all she says.*

The pressure on Abel was around PAF CF/A1. This is the PI which requires CSSRs to report annually *the number of Looked After Children in care for more than six months who have had more than two placement moves in a 12 month period.* The national target which all CSSRs had to achieve by 2003 was that no more than 16 per cent of children should experience more than two moves a year. The logic of this is unimpeachable. The more a child is moved the less likely the child is to settle in a family situation and thrive. Fine, but let's look at the numbers. If a CSSR has, say, 300 children, 16 per cent is no more than 48 of them. Some children are distressed and placements break down regularly. Placements break down for other reasons too. What happens if a foster parent becomes ill, or one foster child bullies or scares another? What if a specialist residential facility is flooded? This could mean several children moved at once. What about large sibling groups where there is a break down? And there have been oddities built into the definition of this PI. Until 2004/2005 adoptions made to families on children previously fostering the same child were counted as placement moves. There were also examples in one CSSR where children at residential school were mistakenly counted as moving placement each time they went home, i.e. about a dozen times a year! But these are 'technical' problems in the sense that they are problems of counting the activity. There are also questionable occasions when a social worker cannot get agreement for a move, even when it is clear that the placement has broken down and is damaging to the child. Abel's case is not hypothetical.

> **Practice Tale 2.** *Beth works in a children's assessment team in the Midlands. Her team has been told that if there's a re-referral of a family situation, or where the situation is not likely to need significant intervention staff should wait until the work is complete before they record the referral so the assessment work can be recorded as if it had taken less than seven days.*

The PI that Beth fell foul of has not been one of the 50 PAF PIs, but one of the other 60, ostensibly less important, indicators that CSSRs are required to report on. One of these requires LAs to report on the proportion of all initial assessments for children completed within seven days. The CSCI act on the assumption that this is a reasonable timescale, although a lot of practitioners and their managers think it is unrealistic. Considerable effort has gone into amending referral and recording processes to meet the seven day deadline, but a great amount of subversive activity occurs as well; not starting the recording of assessments until well into the process, closing cases down even when the work is not complete, or even advice to deal with what seem like small pieces of work completely informally. Beth's experience is not unusual.

> **Practice Tale 3.** *Beth's mother Cath has worked in a Northern county for 25 years and has seen it all. The mainstay of her team, she tends to work with the most difficult older people. Mrs Bothwell has come to the end of her tether in her sheltered housing unit, wanders the streets endlessly whenever she can give her carers the slip, talks loudly through the night to people long dead, never dresses herself properly, is constantly dropping things, flooding the kitchen and even burns herself with hot food from the microwave since her cooker was removed. She has also fainted on two occasions in the last three weeks narrowly escaping serious injury. Cath knows it's time to keep her safe, besides the cost of the care package is beginning to worry her, as is Mrs Bothwell's evident distress. Budgets are devolved and Cath can more or less*

decide the pattern of her workload, so she begins talking to Mrs Bothwell and her niece about a residential placement. But her team leader reminds her that she has placed two older people in residential care in the last two months. 'I'm afraid Mrs Bothwell is going to have to wait' he says, this young team leader in his shiny suit in that portentous way she is beginning to dislike. 'I hinted last month that you were placing too many people'. Cath thought this was a bit rich as it was commonly accepted that in her team she dealt with all the most demanding people. And the way he said it as if she tipped people into care like she was some sort of dog catcher! 'Have you tried respite?' he says. Cath sighs and tries to remain calm. 'That would be cruel' she says eventually. 'It's her neighbours as well as her. They're getting as knackered as she is. She's in danger unless she has someone there all the time. And what would be the point of that? It's time. Don't you see?' 'Well she'll have to wait', says shiny suit, 'the quota's full for this month'.

Cath's PI was *AO/C26, the number of admissions to long term care of older people per 10,000 population*. The reduction in such placement rates has been one of this government's most consistent objectives. Government expects all CSSRs to place less than 120 people per 10,000 of the population of over 65s in long term care each year. For nearly all LAs when the regime was introduced in 1998 this meant they had to reduce the number of placements made. Again the logic is clear. Residential homes have institutional elements, often do little to maintain residents' independence and have much higher rates of depression than in the community. Government funding was allocated with clear expectations that the money should be used to further this objective, thus the establishment over the last several years of post discharge rehabilitation schemes, extra care sheltered housing units and joint work with PCTs around community health services. But the pattern of residential placements varied hugely across the country in 1998. Many councils introduced quotas to ensure they reached their target.

Practice Tale 4. *Back in London Dev can't believe he is having to ring foster parents asking if their hulking great 15-year-old lads have had a medical check in the past twelve months. 'He went to casualty when he got a screwdriver stuck in his hand'. 'No that's not what I mean. I'm talking about a health check . . . you know, going to the doctor to say aahhh and being weighed'. Dev finally persuaded the foster parents but hoped that no one would ask him how these young men were to be persuaded to go to the health centre for such a purpose.*

Dev had been asked by his manager to check whether the young people on his caseload had had a *dental check and Health Assessment during the past year*, PI CF/C19. Once again the logic of this PI is flawless – children in public care should have the same health care attention as children in the general population. Ensuring that these simple checks take place is one way of highlighting that expectation. The problem here is that young people over the age of 14 no longer have 'health checks' as a matter of course at school and besides older teenagers can refuse to go – and they do. Thus the harassment to get this chore done.

Practice Tale 5. *'The review's next Thursday' said Ephraim, a review manager with a North Eastern authority. He was talking on the phone to his Principal Officer. 'Yes of course it's on time. I told you it's on time. We just had to shift it a couple of days'. Silence. 'But we couldn't get everyone there on Tuesday. Roger's on holiday till then and the health visitor's been off with flu. That's why we put it back till Thursday'. He went silent again. 'Surinder, I know all about getting reviews done on time. It's my job. And I know that technically the six months is up on the Wednesday but how the hell can you have a proper review without the social worker there?' More silence. 'What's that? Say that again, I don't think I heard that right'. He went quiet again. 'You want me to date the conference as having happened on the Wednesday? I don't believe it'.*

Ephraim was labouring under the demands of PAF *CF/C20, the percentage of Child Protection Reviews completed within the timeframe*. The timescale for a first review conference is three months after the initial conference and then six months for each subsequent review. The CSCI expects 100 per cent of reviews due to be completed on time; again not an unreasonable expectation for the most vulnerable children in the country. About a third of LAs managed this for 2003/2004 and all but a handful reach 90 per cent or above. This is a more important PI than most, a 'Key Threshold' (a 'KT' – the detail of which will be explained in Chapter 3). In effect KTs are indicators of mass destruction – get them wrong and your star rating goes down. So missing the deadline for a CP review is just not allowed.

Perverse incentive

The impact on these five workers has been various, but in these examples little good has come from the operation of the PIs. They all felt less in control of their workload or less valued in what they did. Some felt that the actions required of them were a waste of time, unethical or potentially dangerous to the people they were working with.

In addition workers will say the tangential impacts of the Performance Assessment Framework have been just as debilitating. More has to be recorded as a matter of course – this means, some say, that more time has to be spent in front of the computer screen than with service users. And while the activities in the examples above make sense if you understand the performance context and PI concerned, many workers are not well enough briefed on the performance agenda and remain baffled by actions they are expected to take. Others report that their time and planned work is high-jacked by urgent demands for particular sorts of activity at odd times – they understand it is something to do with PIs, but it never quite feels much to do with them, or the service users.

Most of all, front line workers point to the crudity of the PIs. So while it might seem sensible that the number of Looked After Children who achieve one GCSE grade A–C (PAF *CF/A2*) is counted, many social workers are aghast that the Government expects 50 per cent of Looked After Children to achieve that. And of course there are many PIs which critics suggest create perverse incentives – achieving the opposite of what is intended or affecting other service outcomes adversely. So with PAF *AO/C28 The number of Older People receiving 10 hours a week care and six visits or more a week*, social workers in some LAs have claimed they are encouraged to add a couple of unnecessary care hours onto a package just to reach the magic ten hours. 'What does that mean?' a social worker said to me. 'That's more likely to make a person dependent not independent. It's just jumping through hoops for the PI'. Another said, 'we've lost sight of the service user in all this – we're just doing these things to feed the machine' and yet another, 'senior managers don't care about us or the clients . . . just these stars'.

These front line concerns are well known. An Audit Commission (AC) report on the introduction of performance measurement admitted that it had only partly worked (Audit Commission, 2002). This was a general review across all local authority functions, but accurately identified many social care concerns. The AC reported that managers expressed several frustrations: that they were pulled in too many different directions by the demands of individual PIs; that their leaders were not interested in how they put performance measurement into operation (as long as the reported performance was OK); that there were too many PIs; that the system was poorly thought out; that staff did not understand that they had to 'change'.

One of the regular comments of front line staff is that this emphasis on PIs is only a fad and will go away. But the CSCI, responsible for the process, is determined to refine and improve the system rather than scrap it and in the wider world performance measurement disciplines are ubiquitous. So we have a paradox, a set of processes that are being strengthened in central government and at senior level in social services departments, but which are treated with suspicion by many professionals involved at the front line.

The aim of this book is to explore the apparent dissonance between the government's enthusiasm for performance measurement and performance assessment and the less than comprehensive engagement of many front line staff. The next chapter charts the rise of the use of performance measurement disciplines in the public sector and its current national context. Then I will outline the detail of the current system. This is followed by an analysis of the system. Finally there is a discussion about how front line staff can make best use of the current processes and how those processes could be improved.

Exercise: Managing your own performance

It might be useful in your thinking to begin by identifying your own experience of attempting to improve your performance. You can do this on your own or in your team:

1. Think of an activity for which you were trying to improve your own or a group's performance. It doesn't matter if it's work or play – the inexorable rise of a netball team you were in, the improvement in a new work skill or becoming a more accomplished darts player. What was it about the way you tried to improve that worked? And was it the external pressure of the looming maths exam that concentrated your mind or a personal obsession with learning to paint better? Research indicates that there are two broad types of goal perception; an ego orientation, where winning is the important thing and task orientation in which people value enhanced competence for its own sake. What are you most driven by, external demands or inner pressures?
2. Then think back five years to what you were doing then – whether it was in social care or not. At that time how was the success or otherwise of your team or your individual work judged and who made the judgement? If you worked in a regulated service what the Inspection Unit said may have had some impact, but what about your managers – what did they say about you or your team's performance?
3. Finally when Friday comes how do you know you have had a successful week? What are the critical success factors for your work?

Chapter 2

The Context of Performance Measurement and Performance Assessment

Choice and internal markets

In April 1985 the *Today* Programme on BBC Radio Four introduced regular business reports, following the introduction of the FTSE 100 the year before. Until the early 1980s the news profile of the stock market and 'business' had been relatively low. Only strikes, closures and big takeovers had made headlines. The government's agenda held concerns about business activity as secondary to other issues. The post war consensus had been, in effect, that the first duty of government was funding and expanding the welfare state. And this expansion had attracted young talent into local government and regular increases in funding. But this began to change with the 1973 oil crisis. Arab oil producers decided for the first time to use oil production as a political weapon against the west. The constriction in supply led directly to tax rises in Britain, an embarrassing plea for a loan from the International Monetary Fund in 1976 and cuts in public service expenditure. The Labour Prime Minister Jim Callaghan admitted in 1977 that the 'party's over'. The party in question had included, according to the critics, state handouts to ailing manufacturing companies, an ever expanding benefits bill, inefficient state monopolies, and powerful unions which vied with managements to direct the purpose of companies. All this drew sharp criticism from those who saw unfettered 'wealth creation' as the way to maintain long term prosperity. The criticisms are encapsulated in a comment by Michael Heseltine, a Conservative minister in the 1980s.

> By 1979 local government had become a barely controllable free-wheeling employment machine which for year after year had been run largely for the benefit of the machine-minders.

Ball and Monaghan, 1993.

Successful companies, it was argued, kept workers in jobs, paid the taxes for welfare services and provided the wealth for affluence to trickle down to those less successful. This critique was harnessed by the Thatcher government (1979–1990) with consequences for social services and for the whole of local government.

It is worth emphasising that the pressures on local government and social services that seem so characteristic of the Thatcher era were only partly a result of government policy. Until the 1970s local government had been a delivery mechanism for government policies in a stable social environment, service delivery being seen as the core of its function. Another key feature was the professional leadership which had dominated local government since the war. But in the 1970s society was changing. Cotton, shipbuilding and steel towns had lost their old dominance and the urban landscape recreated after the war was becoming less predictable. The rise in unemployment, the increased profile of minority ethnic communities, changes in family patterns and the increased use of illicit drugs brought into question the efficacy and manner of local authority service delivery. And the professional leadership in local authorities was accused of having delivered decaying tower blocks, spaghetti junctions, stiff 'wait you're turn' attitudes to basic amenities and in social services the death in 1972 of Maria Colwell.

The notion of performance management would not have been understood in local authorities or social services departments in the 1970s. Outcomes of social care activity were seen in very personal terms by both agency and staff. It was work with individuals or families which counted . . . as interpreted by individual workers themselves. And the overall impact of the organisation's work was not collated and reported on outside the organisation. It couldn't be. Data was kept, collated and reported to central government, but only the activity – caseloads, number of referrals etc. This was built up manually (and painfully) from hard copy records kept by front line staff. Furthermore, social workers and other social care professionals saw themselves much more as direct advocates of service users – sometimes confusing their own aspirations for improved services and extra funding with the needs of the people they were working with. This was part of the social work professional view that social service provision, the mere existence of it, was the mark of a civilised society. As Martin Davies observed of the British social service structure in 1985 this 'humane approach to social policy has had an impact on . . . society that should not be underestimated' and 'social work can only be understood by observing what it does and then by reflecting upon the contribution that those activities make to the way society ticks' (Davies, 1981). But the more general view recognised no desire for social services to make any 'contribution' to society. Social care organisations were one of the discreet cleaning sponges of society – whose role was soak up distress, disability and ill treatment rather than engage in any more proactive relationship with the public. Neither of these attitudes sat well with the business results and efficiency ideas of the incoming government in 1979.

The Thatcher revolution began slowly in the early 1980s, with minor amendments to the tax regime. Deregulation of commerce followed, most spectacularly with the re-launch of the Stock Market in 1987. Procedural changes allowed traders to operate with much less government supervision and fewer controls on credit. Streamlining of the money markets and share trading began to deliver considerable profits to those involved and gave the government confidence to expand its experiment to business. Direct support for industry was cut, trade union powers were curtailed, and from the mid 1980s state industries were privatised. By then the Conservative government was ready to introduce the lessons learned from deregulation into public services.

The underlying analysis of local authority services in the Thatcher and Major administrations from 1979 to 1997 was that these monolithic organisations using bureaucratic control methods were inherently inefficient and were run by people (trades unions and professional groups) for their own advantage. To break this pattern the government oversaw the introduction of four themes into public services. These were:

- The outsourcing of services previously only provided directly by local authorities (or 'in house' as it came to be known).
- Management disciplines in place of professional leadership, opening up local authorities to ideas from the wider commercial world.
- Choice for citizens – in place of universal 'one size fits all' services (see Stewart, 2000).
- Financial stringency – to improve economy and efficiency.

The practical emphasis, whatever the rhetoric, was always on the last. Grant distribution was changed and rate capping powers were introduced for over-spending councils. However, social service finances were not savagely cut between 1979 and 1997. Social services followed the general public service pattern and finances, though not buoyant, were subject to tighter scrutiny rather than reduction. The dance of financial survival each year became central to the work of social services departments.

Many of the ideas introduced to public service related directly to financial stringency. Under the 1982 Local Government Act each local authority had to make proper arrangements for securing services effectively, efficiently and with economy – which became known as the 'Three E's'. Some local authority services, particularly those reliant on low skill occupations – cleaning, refuse, grounds maintenance and so on – were seen as expensive compared to what the private sector could deliver. And indeed pay rates, pensions and associated benefits were generally better than in private industry. So the government identified several services in the NHS and local government that became subject to a compulsory tendering process. Although the primary aim of Compulsory Competitive Tendering (CCT) was to break up inefficient monopolies a subsidiary aim was to save money.

As the Thatcher government became more confident, targeted approaches were developed to lever in market disciplines to health and social care to mimic the 'real' world of commerce. But the mechanisms used for these ideas were an organisational compromise. Government policy makers never quite got the courage together to float the NHS and social care organisations into the commercial world. Instead 'internal markets' were created. So GPs, contracted to the NHS, could become 'fundholders' and 'purchase' services from other clinicians, who were also part of the NHS. Similar arrangements were introduced into social care services for adults and older people. The bureaucratic effort required to make the new processes work was accompanied by a determination to 'embed' these ideas within public service organisations. So, to some extent, the introduction of market disciplines changed the way people working in social care thought. CSSRs began to adopt such titles as 'business units' for internal sub sections. Training in management disciplines was introduced and the fashion for public sector managers to follow MBA courses began. The government helped confirm such attitudes by establishing carefully named guardians of the probity of public service in the Audit Commission (AC) set up in 1982. Many public organisations had new leaders appointed who knew little about the service in question, but had strong business backgrounds. Most famously Derek Lewis, who had worked in the media, took over the prison service for three short years before being ousted by the Home Secretary, Michael Howard, after a series of spectacular prison escapes.

A steady drip of propaganda accompanied these changes. The supporters of the Thatcher government decried the traditional 'anti-business, anti-entrepreneurial streak' they saw across the British social landscape and tried to reverse this. Strong doses of raw and aggressive language were directed at public services. This from Nicolas Ridley, a government minister:

> The root cause of rotten local services lies in the grip which Local Government unions have over those services . . . Our CCT provisions will smash that grip once and for all. The consumer will get better quality services at lower cost.

Local Government Chronicle, 1989.

As a result wage rates in public services slipped, public service organisations became less desirable as employers and social work in particular attracted fewer people to CQSW training – especially men. Social work was not attractive to a generation beginning to be imbued with business machismo. But this new toughness appealed to quite a few public service managers. And so it was that by the early 1990s many working in senior positions in public services were aping private sector managers – even to the point of wearing red braces!

But despite talk of the consumer and quality the overwhelming emphasis was always on financial stringency in both central and local government, pushing any concerns for outcomes for service users or overall performance aside. The Efficiency Unit (A Cabinet Office review body) admitted as much in 1988:

> *Pressures on departments are mainly on expenditure and activities: there is still too little attention paid to the results to be achieved . . .*
>
> Cabinet Office Efficiency Unit, 1988.

The balanced scorecard

During the same period leading companies across the western world were questioning their reliance on finance as the primary arbiter of business achievement. This led through the 1980s and spectacularly in the early 1990s to a re-evaluation of what was important in achieving and maintaining commercial success. A couple of stories illustrate the nature of a long running crisis of confidence. From the late 1960s Japanese motor bikes, cars and electronic equipment had been appearing across Europe and the United States. Mocked at first as cheap copies, the durability and quality of Japanese products took the west by surprise. How could the Japanese make high quality products so cheaply? Whole industries went out of business – the UK motorcycle industry for instance – before companies began seriously looking at what was happening. Xerox, the electronics giant most associated with photocopying equipment, was alarmed in the late 1970s by the market being flooded with high quality photocopiers at much cheaper prices than their own. They decided to look in detail at this competition. Xerox not only picked apart the machines but investigated work practices too. And they looked at a range of products, not just one. Although hardly an innovation Xerox formalised the process of testing their products and processes against the best and this practice of 'benchmarking' became a key feature of the revival of western business confidence. One of the things that Xerox found was an extraordinary set of work practices in Japan, which relied on two principle elements. First of all, the people on the conveyors and wiring components together were often encouraged to comment on work processes and propose improvements, which were then adopted. This relied on mutual respect and the inculcation in the workforce of the belief that they were part of the whole team. This was a far cry from the widespread command and control systems western manufacture was run on. Secondly, procedures were built into the manufacturing cycle ensuring that defective items were spotted before coming off the conveyor and arrangements were made to improve the process that led to the poor product in the first place. So 'quality control', an end of conveyor process, with consequent loss of defective items, was replaced by 'quality assurance', activity built into every process along the whole cycle. It became obvious that these Japanese companies were attending to every last detail of their design and production process. Western companies followed suit. The resultant Total Quality Management (TQM) movement dominated the commercial landscape by the late eighties. Part of the TQM ideal was to focus attention on the whole process from design to after sales service. As such the customer and the attempt to make the product fit for the customer's purpose was seen as much more important in the manufacturing process. Thus marketing and market research, previously back room affairs, came blinking into the light to become highly respected parts of the product development process.

So while in the public sector in Britain in the late 1980s financial disciplines were the predominant import from the private sector, in the private sector itself more imaginative ideas were developing. Some of these ideas slipped into the public sector. There was a public sector version of Management By Objectives. This was largely interpreted in the late 1980s as a personal appraisal tool and became the mechanism whereby performance related pay was offered to senior people. In practice the objectives set were limited and the performance related pay often became an automatic bonus. Ideas about 'quality' entered public service parlance too, accompanied by the introduction of a range of quality standards. The most well known and long lasting of these was the Investors in People award (introduced in 1987), which recognised organisations with minimum human resource standards. The Audit Commission during the late 1980s began to encourage government depart-ments to establish measures of how well they were performing. York City Council (a district authority at the time) developed in 1989 a range of performance indicators to gauge progress against manifesto commitments.

But these ideas did not unseat the dominance of the financial bottom line. Of course if a company does not turn in a profit or cannot foresee turning in a profit the company goes bust. But the focus on the annual profit figures in companies was often to the exclusion of all else. During the 1980s businessmen and academics began to question whether annual profit figures should be their only master. Companies have often failed for other reasons than immediate profitability. Gerald Ratner famously destroyed his jewellery company by implying his customers were fools when he proclaimed his products were 'crap'. Firms sometimes lose the knack of anticipating public taste, as, it has been suggested, Marks and Spencer has done. The British coal industry, although producing clean, high quality coal efficiently was, in effect, wound up by its owners, the government, due to a perceived political threat from the workforce.

Criticism of the overwhelming primacy of earnings based judgements about success began to crystallise in the early 1990s, most famously in the work of two academics, Robert Kaplan and David Norton. Their seminal 1992 essay *The Balanced Scorecard; Measures that Drive Performance* (Kaplan and Norton, 1992) suggested that profit figures were:

- So high profile a measure that it was tempting for managers and companies to misreport actual performance.
- The results of yesterday's decisions, and therefore offered no planning potential, thus they reinforced short term perspectives.

Kaplan and Norton's solution was to propose measuring organisational performance in four key areas of activity; finance, customer response, internal business processes, and how the organisation learns and grows. To map and integrate these four areas they used a simple diagram; the balanced scorecard (See Figure 1). To produce the scorecard the overall strategy and plans within each of the four key areas have to be identified by senior managers. Then goals and measures have to be identified for each and methods of measurement for each identified. The overall plans are translated into sub plans and goals for each level or group in the organisation. Each manager down the line has responsibility for communicating the goals within his or her section of the company. The next stage is to identify a plan for each section and identify targets to meet the goals for each of these sections. Throughout the year data is collected and progress measured against the goals, lessons learned and plans revised for the following year. So a range of activities were incorporated into a planning process, providing milestones of progress and warning of anything going wrong in any aspect of the company performance. Once companies were using this process Kaplan and Norton undertook research into its effectiveness. They suggested that the main uses of the scorecard are:

- Clarifying and updating strategy;
- Communicating strategy through the company;
- Aligning unit and individual goals with the strategy;
- Linking strategic objectives to long term targets and annual budget;
- Identifying and aligning strategic initiatives;
- Conducting periodic performance reviews to learn about and improve strategy.

The beauty of the balanced scorecard is that it integrates the activities of all and identifies the role of each group and individual within the organisation. The idea took off immediately. The speed of this take up is explained by three factors. First of all the underlying idea is so simple; possibly dangerously so, as it can reduce complex activity to a crude formula. Secondly, use of and

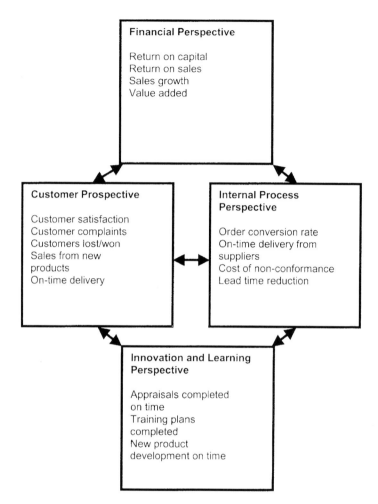

Figure 1　Kaplan and Norton's Balanced Scorecard

discussion about the balanced scorecard requires no recondite knowledge. You don't have to be a TQM specialist or have a Masters in marketing to see where you fit into the overall plan. Thirdly Kaplan and Norton introduced the balanced scorecard at exactly the right time. By the early nineties the availability of the internet, spreadsheets and databases that could be used by literally anybody meant that data storage, transfer, calculation and interpretation were no problem – no longer were these processes the property of specialist research sections. It is also flexible and there are now many versions of the balanced scorecard approach. Perhaps the most well known in Britain is the European Foundation for Quality Management (EFQM) model (See Figure 2). This has three key themes, **inputs** (with four sub-sets), **processes** (the engine which turns inputs into outputs) and **outputs** (with four sub-sets).

These ideas quickly established themselves as the *sine qua non* of planning and performance management across commerce and manufacture. Commentators have suggested that by the year 2000 between 30 per cent and 60 per cent of companies used some sort of balanced scorecard and that 85 per cent used some version of performance measurement (Rigby, 2001).

Soon public service organisations joined in. For unlike so many other management notions, the barriers to the application of the ideas underpinning the balanced scorecard in public service were surmountable. Robert Kaplan himself outlined six problems in introducing such ideas into US public service, all of them recognisable in Britain:

- Within city and state authorities there are several 'businesses' each with different oversight bodies with different interests and agendas.
- There were relatively few incentives to take a long term view of performance.
- The need for public disclosure of business activity reinforces fear of failure.
- There is within public service limited ability to offer financial incentives to high performing managers.
- Outcomes are difficult to measure.
- Achieving desired outcomes requires effort from several different departments and organisations that traditionally work in their own domain (Kaplan, 2000).

Determined efforts have been made to confront and overcome these barriers, and in the US cities like Charlotte Mecklenburg in North Carolina have established considerable reputations on the back of their use of the balanced scorecard (see the current strategic business plan for the city of Charlotte Mecklenburg at www.charmeck.org).

So immediately influential was Kaplan and Norton's work that in the US the Clinton administration (1993–2001) supported legislation (the Government Performance and Results Act 1993) requiring each local authority to operate a version of it and report performance against a range of activities on an annual basis. There had been many performance measurement initiatives previously but this legislation made an orderly approach to it unavoidable. For a fascinating discussion of the beginnings of performance management in US public services (see Osborne and Gaebler, 1992). It is this legislation which the Blair administration in Britain drew on for some of the content of the 1998 White Paper *Modern Local Government* and the Performance Assessment Framework adopted by the Department of Health for social services performance reporting in 1998.

Only Get Better?

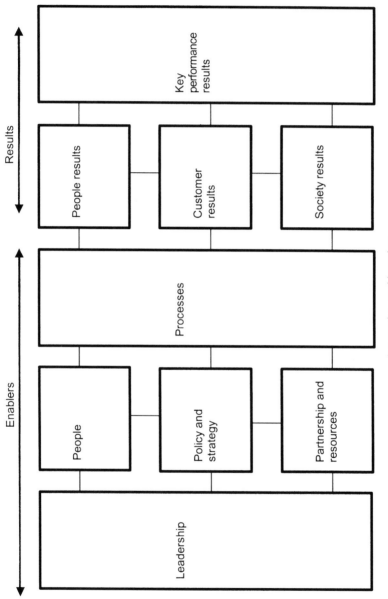

Figure 2 EFQM Model Scorecard (from www.efqm.org)

Establishment of the current performance regime in social care

Before considering how these ideas were played out in Britain it is worth noting the impact of the innovations of the Thatcher/Major years on the work and performance of social services. In narrow terms the emphasis on financial disciplines worked, as costs were curtailed. But although there was constant grumbling, social work practice was in the main unaffected. CCT for instance did not directly affect social care delivery and efficiency savings restricted services rather than changed the way they were offered.

Practice developments continued throughout the period. In children's services the 1989 Children Act was enacted. Its aim was to 'strike a balance between the rights of children to express their views on decisions made about their lives, the rights of parents to exercise their responsibilities towards the child and the duty of the state to intervene where the child's welfare requires it' (The Children Act 1989; Guidance and Regulations, 1990). The Act set out a comprehensive legislative structure across child care activity and established a clear practice framework. This had been influenced by the several child death enquiries during the 1980s and, in broad terms, was welcomed by practitioners. The thrust towards emptying and closing long stay institutions for people with learning disabilities and people with mental health problems, set in train in the 1970s, was beset in some parts of the country by financial problems, but the process continued and in some places gathered pace. And for children, learning disability and mental health practice developments heavily influenced policy.

On the other hand there was little pressure to unpick ageing CSDP Act processes for adults with physical disabilities, such as the assessment and delivery of community equipment and funding telephones for vulnerable people. These old fashioned processes were left alone by the government.

For older people the story was different again, ideology and cost driving change. Financial pressures on the NHS led to a steady closure of long term wards for frail older people, who were then placed in residential or nursing homes. This created considerable pressure on the local authority residential care sector. Then a simple administrative change made to benefits regulations in 1981 entirely changed the landscape. From then on the Department of Social Security (DSS, the government department responsible for benefits) could pay for older people without funds to live in private residential homes. This was seen as a way of taking the pressure off local authority owned residential homes, which were having to operate waiting lists, so great was the demand. It also fitted the free market philosophy as it was thought the market of private sector homes would be stimulated and expanded. This juxtaposition of choice for older people and private enterprise responding to that choice worked spectacularly well. Funding places in private homes for older people cost the exchequer £100m in 1982. Ten years later the annual bill was nearing £2,000m, so much money in fact that alarm bells rang in Whitehall at the spiralling cost. The response, in the form of the 1990 NHS and Community Care Act, attempted several things. First of all the DSS funding for older peoples' residential care needs was incorporated into social services budgets. The social services task became the assessment of the needs of older people and commissioning services to meet those needs. In effect their task was to 'gatekeep' applications for residential care and choke off the uncontrolled demand. The leverage to bring down overall costs was crude, in that the funding allocated from central government never matched what had previously been spent by the DSS on residential care placements.

As demand for residential placements remained high and little imagination was used either by CSSRs or central government about offering different responses to the demand the number of residential placements continued to rise. Financial ends were made to meet in most CSSRs by raising the thresholds for eligibility for care, which led to the complete eradication of simpler services for older people, such as home cleaning. Thus the greatest success for 'choice' and the mixed economy of care across all health and social care in the 1980s led to a resurgence of institutional style care and the eradication of home care for people with moderate needs when just the opposite was being urged for other service user groups. And this one real success for choice in social care had to be constrained because it was too expensive.

In fact in the 1980s and 1990s few lessons were learned within CSSRs from the private sector about managing complex social care businesses – although a lot was learned about financial management in hard times. And until the early 1990s the idea of performance management was hardly developed in social care. Had social services managers been asked about performance management until the late 1990s they would have reached for the budget figures or the complaints file and probably not considered anything else.

But the idea of the performance indicator was creeping into public service in a piecemeal way, designed to deal with particular issues rather than as part of a comprehensive performance approach. The introduction of the Financial Management Initiative in 1983 incorporated the aspiration that managers at all levels should have a clear view of objectives and the means to assess and wherever possible measure outputs or performance in relation to those objectives (Carter, 1989). But government departments were encouraged to develop indicators rather than obliged to use them. And no national PI set was identified for any public service. As their use crept in immediate criticism was made about central government's use of them as a crude control mechanism.

The first direct performance indicators introduced into the NHS, in 1985, were, according to Peter Smith, an attempt to 'enable central government to secure closer control over devolved management'. This particular scheme's emphasis was on measures of managerial processes (Smith, 1993). Smith's study of how rates of perinatal mortality were reported by managers responsible for maternity units identified a set of pitfalls and temptations for managers whose task was to report progress against specific performance indicators. The seven pitfalls identified by Smith were:

- **Tunnel vision.** The temptation for managers to concentrate on the areas of activity included in the PI to the exclusion of others.
- **Suboptimisation.** The pursuit by managers of their own narrow objectives at the expense of strategic co-ordination.
- **Myopia.** Concentration on short term issues, to the exclusion of longer term outcomes.
- **Convergence.** An emphasis on not being exposed as an 'outlier' (i.e. noticeably worse or better than the field) on any PI.
- **Ossification.** Due to the focus on the PI a disinclination to experiment with new and innovative methods.
- **Gaming.** Altering behaviour just to gain advantage in relation to the PI rather than the real outcome.
- **Misrepresentation.** Cheating.

Smith found that managers of maternity units admitted to all bar the last. This early critique of the impact imposed performance indicators is not significantly different from current views.

Another manifestation of central control, according to the critics, was the establishment of inspection bodies for services previously controlled by professional activity. The most famous example here is Ofsted (The Office of Standards in Education), which greatly expanded the function of HMIs (Her Majesty's Inspectors) and replaced the oversight previously given by local authorities. The introduction of 'arms length inspection' for both private sector and in house social care services, as part of the Community Care Act replaced earlier uncoordinated arrangements. The impact was on residential units initially and the results were reasonably consistent across the country. However the process was about checking that rules were being obeyed rather than encouraging improvement; staff numbers and room sizes rather than softer qualities like service user's experience (Lawton and Rose, 1994).

But then the Major administration set in train the processes which formed the basis of the performance measurement and assessment regime of the early twenty first century. John Major's 'big idea' was the Citizen's Charter, which he wanted ' to be one of the central themes of public life in the 1990s' (Lawton and Rose, 1994). The Citizens Charter represented the most systematic attempt yet to make explicit what users of public services could expect from them. The Citizens Charter identified the themes of quality, choice, standards and value and set out six principles which all public services should aspire to. These were to:

- Set, monitor and publish **standards** and publish performance against those standards.
- Produce and publish clear **information** about how services are run, how much they cost and how well they perform.
- **Consult** with users of services, take account of their views and offer **choice** where possible.
- Ensure staff are **courteous and helpful** and offer equity of access to services.
- **Put things right** if mistakes are made and offer simple complaints procedures.
- Provide services which are **value for money**.

The consequent Local Government Act of 1992 required the AC to identify sets of performance indicators for each local authority run service. For the first time local authorities were given lists of PIs which they were obliged to collect, collate and report. They also had to have the results published in a local newspaper (Audit Commission, 1992). There were some PIs introduced then (for the year 1993/94) which are still part of the PAF set including PAF CF/A1 *the number of placement moves for Looked After Children* for instance and the PAF AO/C29 to C32 *series, the number of disabled people helped to live at home* by each authority.

The AC itself had doubts about all this, suggesting that there were 'too many indicators to be of interest to citizens . . . too few to reflect complex services [and] insufficient indicators of effectiveness, quality and efficiency' (ibid.). At the time independent criticism of these PIs was that they were centrally devised and therefore 'cut across local priorities, might be misused or misunderstood and that the cost of collection might outweigh the benefits' (Rodrigues, 1992).

The Citizen's Charter initiative was ambitious – covering the whole of central and local government. It shifted the focus away from finance and market disciplines towards the needs of the individual citizen and the fitness of the organisation to meet those needs. It is the latter which is the key feature of what came to be the basis of the current public service performance regime. But the mechanisms introduced in 1992 to ensure services met standards were weak. Charter Mark assessments for instance, undertaken to check if services met the standards, were applied for on a voluntary basis. And although performance against Citizens Charter PIs was made public the consequences of poor performance were limited. No overall conclusions were drawn from performance against these PIs about the ability of local authorities to meet the needs of the citizens. So local authority responses to the new expectations were low key. Local authority PIs tended to be seen as the business of central units not operational managers. There was no reason for front line managers to be bothered with PIs which didn't say much about the service and had few consequences. So this framework without compulsion had limited impact.

But this shift away from purely financial and ideological approaches to local government was followed up within social services by the introduction in 1996 of Joint Reviews. In the 1980s the government had transformed the Social Work Service (a professional advice service for CSSRs) into the more regulatory focussed Social Service Inspectorate (SSI). The SSI inspection regime had not attempted complete inspections of CSSRs. Their annual programme only included inspections of small sections of the CSSR, with each authority hosting, in the main, one or two inspections a year. The SSI was not staffed for anything more demanding so its impact on practice was nowhere near as high profile as Ofsted. In the mid nineties the government decided that the SSI did not have the ambition to pinpoint the faults of social services, so the AC was brought in to join the SSI to undertake comprehensive inspections. Joint Reviews were shared inspections of the whole social service operation and all CSSRs were to be reviewed over a five year period. The council being inspected had to provide a comprehensive position statement with supporting evidence. This was followed by fieldwork for the inspection which took a week or two, carried out by up to eight inspectors. The reports of Joint Reviews were made public. Shallow as this approach might appear for multi-million pound operations it was by far the most incisive investigation of social services to date. But the real power of Joint Reviews was they offered a rating as to whether the CSSR was fit for purpose.

The stated aims of Joint Reviews were to 'improve social services by identifying and promoting policies . . . and practice which are achieving better outcomes and better value'. Their starting point, clearly related to Citizens Charter thinking, was that 'people will get a good deal from their social services only when authorities fit services to people rather than slot people into services' (Audit Commission, 1998). The methodology adopted for Joint Reviews led to an overall judgement of how well the CSSR was serving the public made up from judgements about four aspects of performance:

- Meeting individuals' needs.
- Shaping better services.
- Managing performance effectively.
- Managing resources to deliver value for money and quality.

ibid.

The 'managing performance' aspect of this was an ungainly collection of issues including complaints, use of quality standards and regulatory frameworks, the management of directly provided services and the use of targets and target setting.

The language used by Dr Andrew Webster who was in charge of Joint Reviews confirms that the methodology used was developing rather than complete. The focus was on individual authorities rather than on a comparison of performance against national standards. Webster said, 'We don't ask you to measure yourselves against set standards, but against your own standards' (Rho Delta, 1997). The high public profile of these reviews also raised concerns amongst directors (acknowledged by Webster) about whether mischief might be made of the 'output' (ibid.) of Joint Reviews by local politicians. This seems an odd concern now, but the social services community at that time was new to the idea of complete openness about problems or failings. It also confirms that the national agenda was not nearly so dominant a feature of the social care landscape in 1996 as it is now.

About half of all the English CSSRs underwent Joint Reviews, but from 2002 they were discontinued, replaced by the rolling star rating process which I shall describe below. The problem with Joint Reviews was that they were too labour intensive, took place over too long a period to offer any useful comparison between councils and as personnel were different for each inspection consistency was in question. There were questions raised also about the competence of some of the people involved in the reviews. There was no external validation of the Joint Reviews, so these questions from CSSRs, no matter how self serving, remained hanging in the air. And of course each Joint Review produced only a snapshot of how the CSSR was performing – a snapshot only to be taken again five years later. But this snapshot had unpleasant consequences for those CSSRs which did not convince the inspectors of their fitness for purpose. Those CSSRs judged to be 'failing' local people were subject to 'Special Measures' – a notion taken from Ofsted. All this meant in practice was regular reporting to the SSI, with the possibility of 'intervention' if improvements were not forthcoming. Intervention consisted of a team of specialist managers being sent to advise on how to improve things. But the judgement was made public, so the real consequences of a poor Joint Review were on the reputation of the CSSR locally, with colleague agencies, neighbouring authorities and the occasional interested local citizen. The 'failing' Director was usually replaced and managers and staff were made to feel pretty bad too. Apart from being subject to a high profile child death enquiry Joint Reviews established a public profile for poor performance in social services for the first time.

The coming of New Labour

Although it might be suggested that Tony Blair's government of 1997 accepted much of what the Thatcher/Major administrations had done with the economy, this is clearly not the case with local government services. Managers and staff who felt they had been on a roller coaster under the previous administrations may have been forgiven for thinking Labour would give them an easier ride. But local government was Labour territory and the new administration was determined to make it work better. In 1998 a White Paper was published which laid out the future for local government, *Modern Local Government: In Touch with the People* (ODPM, 1998). There were three broad themes proposed: making councils responsive to local people's needs, offering the means for them to make that happen and looking for improvements in the services offered. The focus shifted decisively from efficiency towards improving services by the most effective means possible. One symbol of this was the demand that the old committee system of governance be swept away and replaced with cabinet style governance, replicating the Westminster model. Another was the subsequent identification of a demanding 'e-government' agenda for all local government services (ODPM, 2002). A third was the insertion in the Local Government Act 2000 the requirement that each local authority improve the general well-being of citizens. Such demands, especially the determination that there should be improvements in outcomes for citizens, set a tone of grand ambition for local government absent for a generation.

The primary vehicle identified for driving the hoped for improvement was Best Value, 'a rigorous and systematic approach to improving local authority performance' (DoH, 1998). This short lived regime was established to overcome a major quandary for the new government. The repeal of CCT was a Labour manifesto commitment. CCT had led to the loss of many jobs, severely cut the wages and benefits of many others transferred to private companies and had been seen to be delivering services of variable quality. But the new administration did not want to give out the message that it was content for local government to return to the days of overstaffed and lethargic 'in house' services. Thus in return for the repeal of CCT each local authority was obliged, under the Best Value regime, to 'fundamentally review' all of its services over a five year period. The methodology required each review to incorporate the four 'C's, which were:

Consult. The expectation was that staff, colleagues in partner organisations and most of all service users and citizens should be consulted about the quality of the service, how it worked and how it could be improved.

Compare. Services were to be compared with similar local authority services and any other relevant comparators in private industry, as well as performance of the service being compared with past performance. Thus benchmarking as a regular discipline was introduced across public service.

Challenge. Each review was designed to incorporate a 'challenge' to the status quo. Many different ways of attempting this were used; people from the LA next door were invited to join reviews, as were opposition counsellors and service user representatives.

Compete. The fourth C stands on its own really, as each review team, once they had formed a view of the effectiveness of the service were required to consider whether the task of the service could be achieved in better ways, possibly by seeking to commission it from elsewhere or tendering for it on the open market.

Each review had to operate on an annual pre planned cycle, which was monitored by the AC. At the same time the Department for Local Government, Transport and the Regions (DLTR) introduced a set of Best Value Performance Indicators (BVPIs) for each local authority to report progress against annually (for current Best Value Performance Indicators see www.audit-commission.gov.uk/performance/. The DLTR is now called the Office of the Deputy Prime Minister [ODPM] and has overall responsibility for local government.) The core of these BVPIs were the old Citizen's Charter PIs but included many new PIs – vastly increasing the annual reporting burden. Finally each local authority had to publish a Best Value Performance Plan, which identified how previous plans had worked, what improvements were planned in the coming year and how they were to be achieved. This, in effect, was a comprehensive corporate plan, backed up by PIs, with locally identified targets for all those PIs.

No government document has ever suggested that Best Value failed, but by 2001 it was clear that this largely self regulated pattern of 'fundamental' reviews was not delivering significant improvements. Without strong external pressure it was too much to ask of organisations to completely change the way they operated and to outsource their own services.

Stars

Following *Modern Local Government* came *Modernising Health and Social Services* (DoH, 1999) which was largely about the NHS. This identified national priorities, some shared with CSSRs, thus the title, and introduced the notion of National Service Frameworks (NSFs). NSFs were outlined for several critical and difficult areas of health and social care. The NSFs set national priorities and targets to be achieved within a given number of years, laid down local processes for putting them into practice and reporting mechanisms for identifying progress. Initially the only NSFs incorporating significant social care aspects were the NSF for Older People and that for Mental Health.

A White Paper about social care services *Modernising Social Services* (DoH, 1998) was designed to give the detail of the social care element of the overall health and social care priorities. In the introduction evidence from the 30 or so Joint Reviews which had by that time been completed was quoted as revealing 'too many examples of poor services, widespread inefficiency, and a worryingly high number of authorities with serious or deep rooted problems'. The White Paper set out:

- 'clear objectives for social services'
- 'National Priorities Guidance' with 'key targets for social services to achieve in the medium term'
- resources in the form of a number of grants
- 'effective systems to monitor and manage performance'.

It also claimed that with the 'identification of areas where improvement is most needed . . . it was the first time any Government [had] laid out explicitly its expectations of social services'.

National objectives for both children's and adult's services were set out, with long term targets identified, specific grants offered and a statement made that the Department of Health was 'reorganising its approach to performance management so that it is aligned with and builds upon Local Best Value arrangements'. This confirmed that social care activities would contribute more than before to the overall objectives of each local authority. The performance measurement arrangements included annual reviews of performance, supported by information from 'a new statistical performance assessment framework'. This it was suggested would provide a basis for a 'common understanding between central and local government on performance, value for money and resourcing issues in social services, both at overall programme level and in terms of individual local authorities'.

This Performance Assessment Framework (PAF) (see CSCI, 2005a) consisted of what were described as 50 High Level Indicators of Performance. The stated aims were to gather information about national performance, concentrate effort on particular activities and to compare the performance of local authorities. Government had always collected data on activity from CSSRs, but the PAF represented a considerable extra demand on data collection and collation activity. The PAF also required local authorities to set their own annual targets against all fifty PAF performance indicators (within the context of the national targets). The results were to be made public.

To complete the picture the Quality Protects programme for children's services (launched in 1998) specified precisely what was required of each CSSR and partners and was the vehicle whereby government grants were delivered and achievements checked. This required additional data to be returned annually from 1999. The adult service equivalent, the Promoting

Only Get Better?

Social Services Modernisation Fund	1999/00 (£m)	2000/01 (£m)	2001/02 (£m)	Total (£m)
Promoting independence: partnership grant	253.0	216.0	178.0	647.0
Promoting independence: prevention grant	20.0	30.0	50.0	100.0
Children's services grant	75.0	120.0	180.0	375.0
Mental health grant	46.4	59.4	79.4	185.2
Training support grant	3.6	7.1	9.0	19.7
Total Modernisation Fund	398.0	432.5	496.4	1326.9

Figure 3.   Grant funding made available to CSSRs in 1999. (From *Modernising Social Services*, DoH White Paper, 1998)

Independence Grants, again offered funding for CSSRs to deliver on the national objectives. From April 2000 the DoH required additional data returns for adult services under the heading Referrals, Assessments and Packages of Care (RAP).

This package of objectives, priorities, grants, and targets was easily the most sophisticated attempt to achieve specific service aims ever attempted in British social care. The sums of money in grants announced (see Figure 3) indicate the scale of the government's ambition.

This approach has been the hallmark of New Labour's leadership of the social care agenda, what one manager I know described as 'sweets and finger wagging'.

To a considerable extent the success of this programme was predicated in the government's ability to both understand and then make judgements about what was going on across the country. So the PAF, QP reporting, RAP and the inspection arrangements were crucial. But there may have been other motivations as well. One manager at the CSCI said that initially the PAF was largely about 'cracking the whip' over CSSRs – which were not seen as the most go ahead organisations. And the initial response from CSSRs in the first data collection year 1999/2000, although variable across the country, could be characterised as suspicious, slow and disappointing. This was, I think, for three reasons:

- Underdeveloped capacity for data collection and storage.
- A lack of a language to debate performance with managers and staff in CSSRs.

- A misunderstanding in social services circles about how serious the DoH were about this.

It is obvious that DoH staff were shocked at first by the quality of information returned by CSSRs. It was dire. In many CSSRs collection systems depended on manual returns and sampling of activity across parts of the organisation or parts of the year. There was also much guesswork. Setting targets, a new discipline, was often not done with much rigour. The PI definitions themselves, although carefully considered and logical, often bore the stamp of the statistician. Not many were completely incomprehensible and DoH staff were always very helpful in trying to explain what was required, but a lot of the PIs were interpreted differently across the country, baffling their very purpose.

There was a certain naiveté shown by the DoH in expecting accurate and comprehensive returns, possibly explained by the enthusiasm of their new political masters for IT solutions to everything. It was after all the late 1990s, the very crest of the dotcom boom and Blair's ministers were major evangelists for 'e' everything. I have a view that from their desks in London, with their shiny new PCs, the people creating the PAF in 1998 overestimated the 'e' capacity in CSSRs where staff were just recovering from twenty years of making do with hand-me-down ring binders and buying their own pencils.

Within social services in the late 1990s data collection, collation and interpretation of PIs was often left to IT and information staff and many front line staff were not well informed of what was going on. With limited operational validation of PI data the quality of information reported to the DoH was even worse than it might have been. And let's not forget how alien some of these ideas were to social work staff. A significant barrier to the acceptance of this approach was that front line staff were not ready for it. Apart from staff in regulated services such as residential homes, who were accustomed to inspection activity related to explicit standards, social workers in general operated on a set of values which were, to a certain extent, divorced from organisational demands. Although the notion of professionalism in social work has never been comprehensively accepted, the specific nature of social work training, the existence of a social work community beyond the employer and the emotional demands made, sets social workers apart (in their own minds at least) from their local authority colleagues. The human pressures entailed in front line work, much as in the police service, also provide a convenient fence between front line staff and their direct line managers, who do not have to go out and face the public. What's more, bureaucratic aspects of their task such as keeping statistics, recording, filling forms in and so on, have never been regarded as integral to their work. The folklore for many social workers was that the real job is time spent with service users. This naïve view, as if thinking time, recording, report writing, liaison, persuasion and preparation for interviews are somehow separate from the real task, still permeated the debate amongst many social work staff when the PAF was introduced. And successes in their work, notwithstanding direct outcomes such as a troubled Looked After Child being placed successfully or someone with a learning disability happily settled in her own tenancy, were often measured in very personal terms. So a thank you here, a phone call from a past client, a kind letter from a service user's relative have been regarded as highly by social workers as organisational successes. It's not surprising then, that in many CSSRs the whole PAF programme was not properly introduced to front line staff. With this tradition too the importance of PIs in DoH plans was easy to ignore and the logic of them was not hard to deride as bean counting divorced from the realities of front line work.

This tone changed over the next few years, as the annual PAF report demonstrated which CSSRs were performing well against the PIs and which were not. It was eradicated, in management circles at least, with the introduction of the star rating system in 2002. In May of that year the first judgements were published for both children's and adult services about how well each CSSR was serving local people and what its prospects for improvement were. A related calculation resulted in an overall judgement as to whether the CSSR was a zero, one, two or three star service. Unlike in the days of Joint Reviews the judgements for all 150 English authorities were published simultaneously. In addition those authorities achieving three stars were offered a 'holiday' from service inspections and the ability to allocate grant funding otherwise ring fenced as they wished. But it was not these 'prizes' that gave the process bite. The power in the process was the fear of publicly identified failure. And the clarity of the process (particularly the AA style star rating) made it easily understandable even to members of the public. Authorities judged unworthy of even one star were subject to the 'Special Measures' introduced by the Joint Reviews.

The SSI were careful to say that performance against PIs constituted only a portion of the judgements made about CSSRs and that service developments, outcomes for service users and other aspects of the SSI Standards and Criteria (see CSCI) were equally important. But some CSSRs responded to the assessment by concentrating all their efforts on improving the reported PIs, falling prey to 'tunnel vision' and other of the temptations outlined above. Some CSSRs invested heavily in data collection, performance managers and monitoring, at the expense, it seemed to some on the front line, of proper investment in front line services. Some senior managers argued that good PIs would 'fall out' of good practice. Whatever take each authority had on the process and whatever directors said, the annual performance round quickly became one of the major external drivers for local authority social care organisations.

The introduction of the Corporate Performance Assessment (CPA) process across all local authority functions in 2002 (ODPM, 2001) tightened the screw. The largely self regulatory Best Value system was replaced by a revised national performance management framework, with 'coherent national priorities, stretching targets and the Comprehensive Performance Assessment regime'. CPA Inspections, an authority wide version of Joint Reviews, were introduced on a three year cycle and used a methodology of judgements weighted between the various local authority functions (called 'service blocks'), producing a final decision as to whether a council is poor, weak, fair, good or excellent. Again the consequences for poor councils were a dose of humiliation and senior sackings, while for excellent councils, financial freedoms and inspection holidays followed. This raised the profile of CSSRs in councils for the CSSR star rating contributed directly to the judgement made about the whole council.

The Audit Commission strengthened the whole process in 2005 for the three year period until 2008. The precisely titled *A Harder Test,* in a sense finished the job so tentatively started by John Major 13 years previously (See AC 2005c, www.audit-commission.gov.uk/CPA/Downloads/Oct05CPAThe HarderTest.pdf). All service blocks in each local authority became subject to the same performance assessment regime. Each had identified a set of standards and indicators, and inspection and assessment regimes were introduced if there were none before. These processes allow an annual update of a performance rating for each service block – i.e. environment, housing, adult social care, children's services and so on. The full CPA inspection, as before, takes place every three years, but each authority under *A Harder Test* has to submit an annual submission reporting their 'Use of Resources' and their 'Direction of Travel'. With annual evidence available the CPA rating for all the services in the authority can be updated each year – keeping everybody permanently on their toes. The new CPA moves to a 'star rating' with five possible ratings, zero up to four stars. Several themes underpin the strengthening of the regime:

- Use of the phrase 'standing still is falling back' sends a clear message to all local authorities that the centre expects no complacency in even the best performing local authorities.
- Ratings are made on 'rules based' judgements. This means that there are set standards of performance for each service block. This is a significant change for some local authority functions, as previously the AC published the performance of authorities against many BVPIs in a merely comparative manner.

- Finally the overall CPA rating is calculated using a formula which incorporates the ratings achieved by all the service blocks. In this the 'slowest in the convoy' rule applies, meaning that if any one service block is judged as having a low rating, no matter how good the other service blocks are considered, then the level of the CPA rating is held back.

The disciplines and principles of the inspection regime set up by Ofsted and the performance assessment regime pioneered by the SSI have come to full fruition in *A Harder Test*. Truly now, there is no hiding place. (ODPM, 2005).

As a result of this tightly controlled and increasingly interlocking cycle of activities, councillors and senior managers in CSSRs are bolted into a process which they may have difficulty selling to staff. But they have to follow the drift. The detail of the performance assessment process across local authorities, in health organisations and in social care can be arcane – but the attention paid to health and other government targets during the 2005 election campaign demonstrates that the public has a healthy understanding of the sharpest feature of the process. The government's underlying confidence in the system can be judged by the pace of development in many parts of it, the emerging co-ordination between government departments and a new determination to make the process mean something for service users. Thus the CSCI's current determination to introduce service user outcome measures to replace the current PI set. This matches the approach in the Children Act 2004 and the Green Paper for adult services published in March 2005 *Independence, Wellbeing and Choice*. Both of these espouse a set of outcomes for service users, five for children, seven for adults, which public services have to strive for. The white paper on health and social care in the community due as this book is published will no doubt add more detail to these policy themes. A total review of social care PIs is, as I write, underway to move towards this outcome approach. At the same time the CSCI has become more bullish. The results of the 04/05 Star Rating round in December 2005 were accompanied by the comment that too many CSSRs were 'coasting' (i.e. not striving hard enough to improve). This did not go down well with the ADSS nor did the very low rate of success of the newly introduced appeals process. Forty six CSSRs appealed against their star rating (a third of them!) but only six were successful.

All this might change – it is a political construct after all. There are regular rumours of local government 'shake ups' and fewer PIs. My guess is that it won't change that much and that the administration will build upon the processes developed so far – moulding them to become more subtle and responsive tools. No, the many staff employed in the AC and the various inspectorates (however they are streamlined and reorganised) can sleep easy in their beds at least until 2009.

Summary

In the 1980s and early 1990s, CSSRs looked to the financial bottom line just like the private sector. Adherence to a central policy agenda was maintained by central government's financial stringency and legislation which obliged parts of the CSSR to pretend to operate like a private company. But that's as far as the central agenda went. Ambition to improve services for local people was at first channelled through various mechanisms for improving 'choice' to citizens. However, the Citizen's Charter introduced in 1992 changed the focus toward meeting citizens' needs and ideas such as the balanced scorecard offered a broader view of the potential of planning and perform-ance measurement in the 1990s. Several attempts to harness these ideas failed to deliver improvements in social services; the Citizen's Charter itself, the Best Value regime and Joint Reviews.

Since 2002 CSSRs, led by a tightly set national agenda and explicit national standards, have been focusing on making improvements to a precisely identified set of processes and service outputs identified in the PAF indicators. The mechanisms for ensuring that CSSRs follow that path are based on a rolling analysis of progress, annual public judgements, unpleasant conse-quences for failure and mild benefits for achievement. As we shall see this process has resulted in startling improvements in some outputs for service users. With this and the CPA, government has hit upon a successful set of mechanisms which ensures local authorities follow their lead. Senior CSSR managers are signed up to the logic of this process.

Exercise

Go back to the balanced scorecard chart. For your own team draw up:

1. Your desired outcomes for the people you are serving. (A more compre-hensive exercise might include asking service users what their desired outcomes are). Incorporate the desired outcomes published by your employer. The vision, aims and objectives of your organisation may be a little bland but they will be positive and they will not be much different from anything your team would have devised. But add what specific outcomes your team is striving for.
2. The support you require to achieve those outcomes from HR, Finance, Training, Information, IT, management, supervision, colleague agencies and any other section or organisation which has an input into your team's operation.
3. What you need from business processes to achieve the desired outcomes. This can be difficult to grasp, as well as very complicated, but will include things like operational procedures, decisions points and administrative

back arrangements. For instance how is a piece of work finished? Who decides it is finished? Who records that, how and to what standard? The possible list is endless, so choose key aspects of the processes you rely on.

4. A personal skills audit of all team members. What skills do team members have to bring to the task of achieving the desired outcomes?
5. What the current impact of your team's work is on the people you serve. Numbers, outputs, satisfaction ratings etc.

To undertake these investigations might take considerable time, but I hope you can see the potential of even a limited amount of time spent looking at these issues. Once you have completed as much of these tasks you have time for, subsequent discussion should be around whether what you have identified in 5 is close to what your aspirations are as identified in 1. Do the activities in 4, 3, and 2, combine to produce acceptable outcomes for the people you work for?

Once you have identified the inadequacy of any processes, skills gaps, and resource shortfalls have a look at your team plan. The plan should include proposals to enhance the processes and get your team in shape to achieve the desired outcomes. If it doesn't it needs changing. If you have no team plan you can now create one based on the exercise you have just completed. Obviously resource issues and management approaches to particular problems have to be negotiated with more senior people in the organisation. But being precise about what you need to do to improve your team's work is a good first step.

Chapter 3

The Current Process of Performance Measurement and Performance Assessment

What is performance management?

It might seem odd to pose this question this far into the book, but I hope the reader can see that there are several possible answers. It might mean something different in separate parts of the organisation and there are certainly different levels of activity that contribute to the management of performance.

Most definitions concentrate on the strategic aspects of performance. The Local Government Association (the body which represents local government interests at a national level), suggests the undemanding, though all encompassing:

Performance Management is what you do to maintain and improve the quality of services provided.

See LGA website.

The Improvement and Development Agency (IDeA, a government funded local government management development agency) suggest something even simpler:

What an organisation does to realise its aspirations.

And . . .

It's only purpose is to deliver better quality services to local people.

See IdeA website.

These definitions are commendably simple but face the world helplessly because they give no flavour of what activities might actually be involved. To those on the front line these sorts of definitions have all the appeal of the corporate vision statement. They cannot be expected to engage anyone who doesn't operate at a strategic level. In addition the implication of such simple epigrams is that performance management is not only everyone's responsibility but that it is the core function of the organisation. Marketing people tend to use very similar all encompassing definitions of marketing and Health and Safety people would have us all spend most of our time on H and S issues. Operational staff and managers see marketing and H and S as tiny parts of the overall activity of any organisation and not much to do with them. This is a danger with performance management too unless it is explained a little more fully.

A better definition, in my view, is one suggested by Mike Walters:

Performance management is about the arrangements organisations make to get the right things done successfully. The essence of performance management is the organisation of work to achieve optimum results, and this involves attention to both work processes and people.

Walters, 1995.

Walters' *Handbook of Performance Management* goes on to identify five key activities for performance management:

- Understanding what the overall **purpose** of activity is.
- Setting specific and agreed overall **objectives**.
- Setting clear **performance measures** to underpin the objectives.
- Systematic **checking** of how we are doing.
- Effective **supports** to deliver the objectives – staff, skills, resources.

Still simple and undeniably high level, but with a hint of practicality to go with the ambition. It also contains the key message that performance management has to be a process, a chronological cycle of activity stretching across the organisation, up and down the management line. What this definition lacks however is an explicit planning element.

The CSCI statement of purpose defines the social care performance assessment cycle (rather than performance management as a whole), but it still feels curiously deficient. Included are the aims to:

- Promote improvement in the quality of care to service users.
- Support effective performance management in social care services.
- Provide annual independent judgements of . . . performance.
- Establish what action each council needs to take to improve . . . quality.
- Provide information to service users and the general public about . . . performance.

CSCI, 2005.

It does not include collecting data for use nationally in benchmarking, policy development, and driving forward the national agenda. This may be because of the status of the CSCI as independent from the DoH and DfES and the broader purposes of these government departments.

From these several definitions and the discussions in the first two chapters I have distilled a definition of performance management in social care services. It includes the following:

- The overall aim of the performance management process is to improve services to service users; quality, outcomes, quantity, access and scope. This is to be achieved by:
- Being precise about the tasks of the organisation, the standards required for those tasks and the scope of intended improvement.
- Identifying local objectives for delivery and improvement which incorporate national objectives, partner strategies, local service user needs, staff experience and local knowledge.
- Identifying targets for those objectives using a business planning cycle which employs accurate information about operational activity and staff and financial inputs.
- Ensuring resources, processes and intelligence are in place to deliver the objectives.
- Briefing all involved about the processes.
- Monitoring activity against the objectives and targets.
- Reviewing the objectives, processes and resource allocation in the light of the results of activity and setting new targets and making new arrangements to meet those targets.
- Constantly reviewing the national agenda, local needs and intelligence about activity and outcomes for incorporation into the planning and performance cycle.

But all these definitions imply a comprehensive approach across the whole organisation. They include problem identification and resolution, process analysis and re-engineering, business planning – everything it takes to shift the organisation to improve its outcomes. So these definitions of performance management are grander than most of the activities social care organisations undertake. Although the establishment of a performance management system may be what CSSRs aspire to, what most of them do currently is **performance measurement** which contributes to the external **performance assessment** process.

How does the current process work?

Set out below are the arrangements for England. See Appendix 1 for comment on the different emphases in Scotland, Wales and Northern Ireland.

So performance measurement is a process – interpreted for social care by the DoH, DfES and CSCI as an annual cycle of events. The events in this process incorporate planning, target setting, internal monitoring and external judgement. It is an interlocking cycle. At the root of everything else are the

Standard 1. National priorities and strategic objectives. The council is working corporately and with partners to deliver national priorities and objectives for social care, relevant national service frameworks and their own local strategic objectives.

Standard 2. Social services commission and deliver services to clear standards. Covering both quality and costs, by the most effective, economic and efficient means available.

Standard 3. Effectiveness of service delivery outcomes. Services promote independence, protect from harm, and support people to make the most of their capacity and potential to achieve the best possible outcomes.

Standard 4. Quality of services for users and carers. Service users, their families and other supporters, benefit from convenient and good quality services, which are responsive to individual needs and preferences.

Standard 5. Fair Access. Social services act fairly and consistently in allocating services and applying charges.

Standard 6. Capacity for Improvement. The council has corporate arrangements and capacity to achieve consistent, sustainable and effective improvement in social services. See CSCI website above

Figure 4   CSCI National Standards and Criteria (CSCI, www.csci.org.uk)

national priorities (see CSCI website). The national priorities stood alone in 1998, but appear in each of the National Service Frameworks as they are published. The NSFs are patterns of activity and objectives outlined for separate service user groups. So there is an NSF for mental health, one for children, one for older people and one for 'long term conditions', which includes people with physical disabilities. They are determinedly service user focussed in that they lay out expectations for both health and social care organisations and others. They set overall objectives and targets for implementation over a number of years.

The national priorities are now interpreted by the CSCI for social care by an increasingly sophisticated set of **standards and crtieria** (see CSCI, 2005b).

Each standard sets out how a CSSR should be operating if it is to be judged as 'serving people well overall', the best possible judgement. The standards also indicates how a CSSR will be operating to be judged as 'serving most people well', or 'serving some people well', or 'not serving people well'. So there is a direct link between the priorities, the standards and the judgements available to the CSCI. Related to these objectives and standards is the underpinning data set, the most obvious aspect of which is the **Performance Assessment Framework** and the 50 **Performance Indicators**. All local authorities set out to capture, collate and report data against this data set to the DoH (for adults) and DfES (for children). But the PAF PIs contain a small proportion only of the data annually reported to the DoH. There are a series of detailed reports about specified activity reported to the DoH, eight for adult services and eight for children's. These cover such activities as the numbers of people receiving home care and the number of Looked After Children. There are also a set of secondary PIs which are submitted together in large reports submitted to a formula. For children there is the annual **Self Assessment** document in which CSSRs report progress against the five outcomes required by the Children Act 2004, including education and health outcomes as well as social care outcomes. This Self Assessment is the first stage of an **Annual Performance Assessment**. For older people and adults there is the **Delivery and Improvement Statement (DIS)**. The DIS is for CSSRs to report achievements in the previous year, plans for the coming year, risks and contingencies – across the whole sphere of their activity. Around 80 additional activity and performance measures are reported annually in the DIS. The DIS is often used as a testing ground for new PIs before they are 'promoted' to the PAF. The DIS has been amended for 2006 and requires CSSRs to report the outcomes of their work, rather than the processes reported on previously. Both the children's Self Assessment and the DIS are submitted in May or June each year.

The assessment processes for children and adult services are now slightly different and will continue to evolve over the coming years. For adult services, the CSCI analyse all the data submitted, as well as information from inspections and discuss this with the managers of the authority. There is one main discussion, an **Annual Review Meeting (ARM)** between the Business Relationship Manager of the CSCI and senior managers in the CSSR. The ARM takes place in the summer and concentrates on the reported performance for the previous financial year. But the CSCI are debating with managers in each CSSR all the time. There is *an ongoing dialogue . . . about the overall picture of performance over time and the council's approach to improvement* (see CSCI website). Managers of each CSSR will tell their own tale and 'spin' to their own advantage their reported performance and the prospects of the authority, making great play of their plans to tackle any problems the authority has. The results of the Annual Review Meeting are made available to the CSSR in a letter containing a **Record of Performance Assessment**, which is then discussed within the CSSRs. Suggestions for amendments to the letter can be made to the CSCI and after discussion the wording is agreed. Then the CSCI prepare two judgements about the quality of the services; one indicating how well the authority is serving the public and the other identifying what the prospects are for improvement. An inordinate amount of time is spent validating this nationally. This is for two reasons. First of all the Business Relationship Manager's relationship with the several CSSRs they are responsible for is bound to become close and there may be an inadvertent 'sympathy' develop for their cause. Secondly in the first year of operation there was a regional imbalance in the CSSRs judged to have reached the three star standard. Much grumbling led to a more detailed validation process the following year to ensure national consistency.

The two separate judgements are combined into an overall judgement, using a matrix of rules. The overall judgement, the **star rating**, is published in November, with as much publicity fanfare as social care can muster.

The whole process has since 2004 coincided with the national publication of the 'refreshed' judgement for the whole local authority as a result of the Corporate Performance Assessment. (CSCI, 2005b)

For children the CSCI follow a similar process, but in concert with Ofsted. A meeting between the two inspectorates and the service managers takes place to discuss the self assessment after the Self Assessment document has been submitted in the summer, but is more complicated because services with different structures, traditions and legislation are considered. After that a draft letter is submitted to the CSSR by the inspectorates which can be amended after discussion. Two judgements are made, one about the overall contribution of the council's services to outcomes for children and young people and the other about the council's capacity to improve. Again these are amalgamated into a single judgement. Judgements fall on a four point scale, from Grade 1, 'a service which does not deliver minimum requirements', to Grade 4, 'a service delivering well above minimum requirements. However the CSCI and Ofsted offer *separate* judgements for social care and education. Final judgements are published in November. This process will no doubt move towards a greater level of integration between social care and other council services for children. From 2005 considerable notice was given to CSSRs about these judgements to allow for appeals.

In addition comprehensive inspections of all public services for children are being piloted. These **Joint Area Reviews** will be conducted across all areas from 2006 onwards on a three year cycle.

This process is constantly developing and will, no doubt, continue to change. What changes every year as a matter of course is the detail of the PAF PIs. There are new PIs every year. Old ones are discarded and definitions change. There is logic to this if you are in a position to follow the debate, but from a distance it can all seem arbitrary. For operational staff constant vigilance is required in what activity is important. So don't believe the detail here, it will have moved on by the time you read it. Check it on the various websites identified in the text.

The performance assessment framework

The most concrete part of the cycle, that which impinges most on the front line is the PAF. There is no direct link between PAF 'scores' and the star rating, but there is generally not too much of a discrepancy between CSSRs with 'good' or 'very good' PIs and those with several stars. I shall consider several of the PAF PIs in some detail, but a comprehensive up to date list with definitions can be found at www.csci.org.uk. or on the DoH website at www.dh.gov.uk

Some of what I shall include below about the PAF and PIs refers to arithmetical formulae, and I understand that many people have a slim grasp of statistics. I concede there are comments made below which require basic arithmetical understanding, but no more sophisticated numeracy is necessary. Besides the overall themes that underpin the PAF are the key here not the detail.

As we have seen several of the indicators in the PAF were inherited from the ACPIs which were established in 1993. Others were freshly devised for the PAF and announced in 1998 for the first collection year of 1998/1999. The PIs are set out in three sections. For the year 2005/2006 there are 18 about children's services, 30 about services for adults and one (which measures the number of practice learning days made available for students by the CSSR) about 'management and resources'. The PAF PIs all have precise 'identifiers' (numbers). Those for children and families are identified as 'CF' and those for adults and older people as 'AO'. Each PI then has an identifier letter, A, B, C, D, or E. These refer to the subdivisions of the PAF, the 'domains'. There are five domains:

- National Priorities and Strategic Objectives (PAF identifier 'A')
- Cost and Efficiency ('B')
- Effectiveness of service delivery and outcomes ('C')
- Quality of services for users and carers ('D')
- Fair Access ('E')

These domains mirror the national standards and priorities mentioned above. This deliberate linkage has strong echoes of the balanced scorecard approach referred to in chapter two. The DoH in creating the PAF attempted to link precise sets of activities to each of the standards and thus to the overall national priorities. So the framework created by the DoH offers a clear invitation to CSSRs to pay attention to all aspects of their business across all these domains of activity. The DoH may have expected each CSSR to establish an integrated planning and performance process, incorporating the whole activity of the organisation. Such an approach could help front line staff affected by the detail of PIs to understand those which impinged on their

---

Children's PIs (Key Threshold PIs in italic)

Children looked after
CF/A1 Stability of placements of children looked after (BVPI 49) (KT)
CF/A2 Educational qualifications of children looked after [joint working] (BVPI 50) (KT)
CF/A4 Employment, education and training for care leavers [joint working] (BVPI 161)
CF/B7 Children looked after in foster placements or placed for adoption
CF/B8 Costs of services for children looked after
CF/C18 Final warnings/reprimands and convictions of children looked after
CF/C19 Health of children looked after
CF/C23 Adoptions of children looked after (BVPI 163) (KT)
CF/C24 Children looked after absent from school [joint working]
CF/D35 Long term stability of children looked after
CF/C63 Participation in reviews
CF/C68 Timeliness of LAC reviews
CF/C69 Distance children newly looked after are placed from home

---

Child protection
CF/A3 Re-registrations on the Child Protection Register
CF/C20 Reviews of child protection cases (BVPI 162) (KT)
CF/C21 Duration of the Child Protection Register
CF/64 Timing of core assessments

Children in need
CF/E44 Relative spend on family support
CF/E67 Children with disabilities

CAMHS services
CF/A70 Progress made towards a comprehensive Children and Adolescent Mental Health
Service

Adult's PIs (Key Threshold PIs in italic)

All adults
AO/B11 Intensive home care as a percentage of intensive home and residential care
AO/B12 Cost of intensive social care for adults and older people
AO/B17 Unit cost of home care for adults and older people
AO/C28 Intensive home care (BVPI 53) (KT)
AO/D37 Availability of single rooms
AO/D39 Percentage of people receiving a statement of their needs and how they will be
met
AO/D40 Clients receiving a review
AO/E50 Assessments of adults and older people leading to provision of service

---

Figure 5   PAF definitions for 2005/06

AO/C51 Direct payments (BVPI 201) (KT)
AO/D54 Percentage of items of equipment and adaptations delivered within 7 working days (BVPI 56) (KT)

Older People
AO/C26 Admissions of supported residents aged 65 or over to residential/nursing care (KT)
AO/C32 Older people helped to live at home (BVPI 54)
AO/E47 Ethnicity of older people receiving assesment
AO/E48 Ethnicity of older people receiving services following an assessment
AO/D55 Acceptable waiting times for assessments (BVPI 195) (KT)
AO/D56 Acceptable waiting times for care packages (BVPI 196) (KT)
AO/D52 Older people home care user survey – satisfaction with services
AO/D71 Older people home care user survey – further PI to be announced in autumn

Adults 18<65
AO/C27 Admissions of supported residents aged 18–64 to residential/nursing care

Physically disabled and sensorty impaired adults aged <65
AO/C29 Adults with physical disabilities helped to live at home

Adults with learning disabilities aged under 65
AO/C30 Adults with learning disabilities helped to live at home

Adults with mental health problems aged under 65
AO/C31 Adults with mental health problems helped to live at home

Carers
AO/C62 Services to carers

Training PI (includes children)
MR/D59 Practice learning

NHS interface indicators
AO/A6 Emergency psychiatric re-admissions
AO/A41 Delayed transfers of care
AO/A60 Participation in drug treatment programmes (BVPI)

Figure 5   PAF definitions for 2005/06 (CSCI, 2005b) *continued*

working lives. This 'Russian Doll' method of setting individual PIs within domains, within adult's or children's services, within national objectives was clever; the DoH's attempt to help CSSRs to link all parts of the organisation within the same performance assessment framework.

The final section of the PI identifier is a simple number. So PAF CF/C23 is the 23rd PI and relates to the domain 'effectiveness of service delivery and outcomes' for social care for children and families. This particular PI requires that each CSSR report annually on the number of Looked After Children adopted within the year.

What makes a good PI?

The AC has set out features of performance indicators, which are worth considering before looking at the detail of the social care PAF set (Audit Commission, 2000). This advice like much else from the AC about performance management is directed at local authorities in general, and those departments and occupations within the authority which identify their own local indicators. The PAF PIs are externally imposed on CSSRs and there is a limited, though strengthening, role for local PIs in social care. However the AC analysis is a useful benchmark. The AC makes out fourteen characteristics of a good PI, although only twelve are relevant to our concerns. Good PIs, according to the AC, should:

1. **Be relevant to the organisation.** This is self evident.
2. **Have a clear definition.** Again this is obvious but as we will see below with the PAF there are definitions which are not as clear as they at first seem.
3. **Be easy to understand and use.** Jargon should be avoided and any calculation that needs to be done should be simple. A good rule of thumb is to try and explain a definition to someone who knows the business. If the definition cannot be explained to them in a minute then there's probably something wrong with it.
4. **Be comparable with other similar organisations.** This too is self evident. However apart from a few shared PIs with PCTs the Health Care Commission (HCC) and CSCI so far use very different PIs even for similar activity. In addition there are some PIs which are bound to produce different sorts of results in different parts of the country. Unit costs of residential care for instance are not comparable in London with those in the North East of England.
5. **Be verifiable.** Verifiable audit trails of data are a general requirement for all PIs. In these terms an audit trail simply means that the data can be traced back to the activity it is claimed to record.
6. **Be unambiguous.** This refers to several things. The definition needs to be unambiguous . . . but so do the results. Unfortunately there are several PIs where the data from CSSRs seems to the CSCI to be so variable that they cannot understand what the data means. Similarly some simple PIs could conceal ambiguities. For instance, using the number of complaints

received by an organisation as a performance indicator is ambiguous. Small numbers of complaints received might indicate service user satisfaction with the service. But it could also indicate an inaccessible method of making complaints, the suppression of complaints by managers or staff or an attitude amongst service users that the service is so bad that it is not worth complaining. The obverse is true; an increase in complaints might not indicate worsening services, but might be the result of an improved complaints system, a more open attitude towards complaints within the organisation, expansion of services into an area which attracts a more demanding clientele or increased confidence in the organisation as a whole.

7. **Be attributable.** Does the PI measure the true impact of the service? If improvements cannot be 'attributed' to the activity measured by the PI then it is not relevant.

8. **Be responsive.** If a PI only measures one thing it has limited use. CSSRs had to demonstrate in April 2004 that they had a Race Equality Action Plan. As it was a Key Threshold (see below) failure to have done so would have affected the overall judgement about their service. However no CSSR was (in the CSCI's language) 'caught' by this – all 150 achieving the required result. So this had the effect of delivering comprehensive compliance on this one occasion. But it had no more use than that.

9. **Avoid perverse incentives.** Part of the purpose of PIs is to provide an incentive to CSSRs to ensure service or activity under scrutiny improves. If however efforts to meet the target have a deleterious impact on the service or acitvity or other services or activities then a 'perverse incentive' is in play. A classic example of this came to public prominence during the 2005 General Election campaign during the *General Election Question Time* BBC TV programme on 28th April. A member of the audience asked the Prime Minister why it was that she could not book an appointment with her GP more than two days before she wanted the appointment. The relevant PI required GP practices to offer patients consultations within 48 hours of the request. Many practices had responded by identifying a 48 hour window before the proposed appointment within which patients could book appointments – ensuring that all bookings met the criterion. Appointments further into the future could not be booked (that would threaten the PI) and those ringing for a booking further into the future than the 48 hours were told to ring again within the 48 hour window. Result? Perfect response to the PI but patients left frustrated and confused.

10. **Allow innovation.** PIs should not be constructed to deter organisations from devising more effective methods of delivering services. No innovation is allowed with the PAF set so this not does apply.

11. **Be statistically valid.** Again this is self evident.
12. **Be timely.** This refers to the availability of the data. Data available too late in the cycle is not useful for planning.

These characteristics are organisational requirements. Front line staff need clarity of a slightly different order. Performance Indicators attempt to measure how well an organisation is doing against an identified activity. To successfully do that certain things have to be in place. These include:

- A precise idea of what the activity is to be measured.
- A clear idea of what the overall objective is and how it relates to the rest of the work.
- An understanding of how that activity is to be measured.
- A reliable and understandable means of measuring that activity.
- A calculation which produces an understandable result.
- A clear idea of the direction of travel required, so staff know if they are doing things right.
- An understanding of what the results mean.

PAF performance indicators

The most detailed and precise analysis of social care PIs has been by Nick Miller (see Miller, 2004) and Pearce and King (see Pearce and King, 2004). Their work is worth considering for a more detailed analysis of the PAF PIs than is offered here. Below I'll explain the general logic of the PIs in the PAF and then investigate how some of them work.

The most obvious use for a PI is where there are discrete activities which are recorded as a matter of course and where the organisation is clear that more or less of this activity is required to deliver its objectives. As the national priorities include the expectation that more Looked After Children are cared for in homely settings rather than in institutional care it would be useful, wouldn't it, to use as a PI the number of Looked After Children adopted each year? Since 1998 this has been one of the PAF PIs, CF/C23 *Adoptions of Children Looked After* (CSCI, 2005a). This is a prime example of something which should make a good PI. This PI has the added advantage that the numbers are tiny. Even in the biggest authority, the number of Looked After Children adopted in any given year will be less than a hundred, not something that requires a sophisticated database to count. No Performance Indicator could be more straightforward.

But in social care even the simple is sometimes complicated. A number of decisions have to be made before the Adoption PI can be put into operation. Such questions include:

- What counts as an adoption? The date of placement or the court order?
- Which Looked After Children are eligible to be counted? Children looked after for any length of time or does there need to be a cut off date?
- Are all types and ages of Looked After Children to be included or should some be exempt, older teenagers for instance where the possibilities of adoption are remote.
- Should adoptions which break down within the year be counted?
- And should there be any weighting for adoptions within the council area?

The definition for 04/05 was:

The number of Looked After Children adopted during the year as a percentage of the number of children looked after at 31 March (excluding unaccompanied asylum seekers) who had been looked after for six months or more on that day.

With this definition each CSSR has to be able to trace the background of the child, excluding unaccompanied asylum seekers, and to know exactly how long the child has been looked after. The CSSR also has to know the number of children looked after. It also has to be able to differentiate between children at various stages of the process, children subject to full statutory orders, or interim orders, or residence orders. The CSSR also has to know when an adoption order was made. All this has to be recorded somewhere. The recording of the data has to be reasonably timely. If progress against this PI is to be followed through the year a once a year count is not good enough – quarterly or monthly updates are required. All this takes considerable effort.

Over the years the definition of the Adoption PI has become crystal clear but there was confusion at first. Well, not so much confusion as CSSRs reporting what they thought was the case, or not checking with the DoH or other CSSRs as to what might be meant. Counting itself, once a definition has been decided upon may seem very simple, but in 1998 when the regular Quality Protects returns had to be made several CSSRs had difficulty even with letting the DoH know how many children they looked after, or how old they were.

The calculation necessary to produce the result for PAF CF/C23 is:

. . . the number of children adopted, divided by the number of children who have been looked after for six months at 31st March of the reporting year (i.e. the end of the financial year).

So if 26 children had been adopted in your authority out of a total of 312 children who had been looked after for six months at 31st March the calculation required would be 26/312.

The number 26 is referred to as the **numerator** and the number 312 is referred to as the **denominator**. These are the terms used by information professionals, simple statistical terms, but baffling unless you know what they

	England	Met. Districts	Shires	Unitaries	Inner London	Outer London
1998/99	4.0	4.1	4.1	4.7	2.9	2.9
1999/00	4.7	4.7	5.1	5.4	3.4	3.2
2000/01	5.2	5.4	5.5	6.3	3.2	3.4
2001/02	5.7	6.2	5.9	6.6	4.4	3.5
2001/02 new def	6.8	7.2	7.0	7.8	5.2	4.4
2002/03	6.9	7.1	7.4	7.7	5.5	4.4
2003/04 new def	7.5	7.3	7.8	7.9	7.3	5.9
2004/05	7.6	7.5	8.2	7.9	6.1	6.0

Figure 6   Table of results of PAF CF/C23: Adoptions of Children Looked after *Social Services Performance Assessment Framework Indicators 2004–05* (CSCI, 2005a)

mean. The denominator is the total figure of population in question – the number below the line in a fraction. The numerator is the number above the line in a fraction – indicating in this case the number of people subject to the required activity. The result of this calculation gives you the figure for the PI. It is a percentage, in this case 8.12 per cent. This would mean that your authority was doing well. The national pattern for adoptions of Looked After Children since 1998/1999 has been as outlined in the chart below.

There is a Public Service Agreement (PSA) between the DoH and the ODPM to increase the numbers of children adopted from care nationally by 40 per cent in 2004/05 from a figure of 2,700 in 1999/2000 (ibid.). This in effect requires each council, by 2004/05, to be reporting 7 per cent of all Looked After Children as being adopted. So, in these terms, a result of 8.12 per cent is very good. The small numbers involved however make steady improvement hard to predict. Say six of the 26 children adopted in the year were from one family and something happened to prevent the order for their adoptions being granted. That would make the total of completed adoptions for the year 20, which produces a result of 6.7 per cent. It doesn't seem much different but it is less than the 7 per cent national target.

Variations on the theme

This calculation, producing a percentage where the highest figures are regarded as the best are the clearest and are used for the majority of PIs. Easiest of all to understand are those PIs which require 100 per cent. So the expectation for PAF CF/C20 *The number of child protection conferences completed within timescales* is that 100 per cent is reported. Many authorities manage to do this and we all understand what this means. Another calculation used regularly compares activity within a specific population with the same activity across a general population. Activities and achievements of Looked After Children are often compared with the activities and achievements of the total population of children in the CSSR's area. This uses the assumption that to achieve the broad goal of social inclusion Looked After Children's experiences and achievements should be the same as the general population of children. The same is the case for services offered to people from ethnic minority communities compared with those offered to the general population. Thus, for instance, AO/E47 *Ethnicity of older people receiving assessment* seeks evidence from CSSRs about the assessment service available to people from ethnic minority communities compared with the general population. What is counted and the calculation is simple. The number of assessments made in the year for people from ethnic minority communities who are over 65 is divided by the total number of assessments made in the year for all people who are over 65. Although the CSCI concedes that there may be a greater level of need within ethnic minority communities, the broad goal identified is that the number of assessments offered should be in line with the general population. So the number of assessments in the minority community (as a proportion of that population) is laid at the side of the number of assessments within the general population (as a proportion of the general population). Say one in nine (0.111) of the general population has received an assessment and one in ten (0.1) of the ethnic minority population has received an assessment then the calculation is 0.1 divided by 0.111.

This gives a 'performance' of 0.9 which is the ratio of the assessments in the ethnic minority population compared to the general population. The perfect ratio would provide a 'score' of '1'. Sometimes the CSCI implies that a score of slightly more than or less than '1' is regarded as more desirable, but usually a narrow band of acceptability around '1' is identified. This is difficult to manage if there are a very small number of people in the population under scrutiny.

Other PIs, like PAF AO/C26 *The residential admissions of older people* and PAF AO/C28 *The number of households receiving intensive home care* are expressed as a proportion of the target population, per 10,000 of the population of older people in the former and per 1,000 in the latter. That's why scores of more than 100 are often possible in the PAF.

Different types of PI

It will have been plain from the discussion above that the PAF PIs attempt to measure qualitatively different things as well as measuring activity in different ways. It is useful to be able to distinguish between the different types.

First of all there are **Process** PIs which measure the speed or efficiency of getting the work done. Thus recording the number of reviews done, the number of assessments or the speed with which initial assessments are completed focus on the processes of the social care business. Some PIs measure **unit costs** – but these are discredited because costs vary so much across the country. Then there are **Output** PIs which measure the outputs of processes. Outputs include, the numbers of people admitted to residential care, the number of adoptions made and so on. Outputs differ from **Outcomes** in that outputs are about what the organisation achieves – the output of the organisation's efforts. The outcome of organisational activity currently means desirable outcome for the service user, one which the service user benefits from and approves of. So an increase in the number of disabled people helped to live at home is an outcome . . . or is it? I would argue it is not because the relevant performance indicators measure the accommodation status of the service user not whether he benefits or not. Individuals may loath 'living at home'. Outcomes are only currently tested in the satisfaction surveys which are required in only two of the PAF PIs. Even these are crude indicators.

Proxy PIs are the most subtle. By measuring one thing they indicate another. Thus CF/A1 by measuring the number of placement moves of Looked After Children gives an indication of the stability of the lives of Looked After Children. The CSCI is clear that conclusions about services should only be drawn from bunches of PIs rather than individual PIs. Thus there is a set of indicators about the quality of life of Looked After Children, which measure school attendance, access to computers in their homes, educational attainment, criminal activity and so on. An odd set of indicators they make, most concentrating on very formal aspects of a young person's life. But a child with a computer at home, who attends school, who has good educational attainment and with no criminal record can fairly be said to have better life chances than a child showing the opposite characteristics. So this set of PIs is a reasonable proxy for good life chances.

Good PIs and poor definitions

There are many definitional problems with the PAF set. The full definition for PAF AO/C26 is *The number of older people (aged 65 or over) placed in long term residential or nursing care per 10,000 population aged 65 and over.* This is a bit of a mouthful, but is crystal clear. Isn't it? Even with this seemingly straight forward definition there have been problems. For instance, a move from a residential home to a nursing home was for a long time counted as a new placement – even if the older person completing that 'move' might be staying in the same room in the same home. And for years there was a tiny definitional glitch which allowed many authorities to under report quite legitimately. The old definition assumed placements were made from the community. Long term placements made when the older person was already in residential care on a short term basis could be legitimately excluded from the PI. Naturally, as part of the strategy for recording fewer admissions, the temptation to admit older people to short term care before admitting them on a long term basis was too much for some CSSRs.

There are also PIs which sorely test the capacity of many CSSRs to report accurately. One of the Key Thresholds (see below) is PI D55 *For new older clients the average of (i) the percentage where the time from first contact to the beginning of the assessment is less than or equal to 48 hours (that is two calendar days), and (ii) the percentage where the time from first contact to completion of assessment is less than or equal to four weeks (that is, 28 calendar days).* This complicated definition is designed to test an authority's ability to get on with and complete assessments in a timely fashion. The key technical requirement is the ability to record the beginning and end of assessments accurately. This is some task for even the smallest authority with, say, as few as 2000 assessments and reviews a year to record. The baffling feature of this PI however is the judgement about when the assessment starts. It could be judged in the case of a self referral that the assessment starts at the time of first contact between the citizen and the staff member who spoke to them. But alternatively it might be said to start when the case is allocated to a worker, or when the appointment to see the person is made. In fact the definition for 05/06 is:

> *An assessment or review begins when an authorised professional member of staff commences a community care assessment (under section 47(1) of the NHS and Community Care Act 1990). To commence such an assessment the member of staff must have begun to assess the needs through discussion with the individual and agree with the individual what further action should be taken.*

But does that always mean the worker who carries out the assessment, a professional remember, should be qualified? Does a District Nurse in an integrated team count for instance? The possibilities of interpretation are still considerable. There was so much unease about the potential variation in the interpretation that the CSCI, although still requiring the data to be reported, has postponed making any judgement about CSSR's performance for the first part of the PI.

Key Thresholds (KTs)

Within the PAF set a number of PIs are seen as more important than the others. These generally have related 'national targets'. These more important

Performance Indicator as Key Threshold	Lower Threshold
Children	
CF/A1 No. of looked after children with more than two placement moves in a year.	More than 20% limits maximum judgement to serving 'some' people well.
CF/A2 Percentage of children leaving care over 16 achieving one GCSE (A-G).	Less than 25% limits to 'some'.
CF/C20 Percentage of child protection reviews completed to timescale.	Less than 92.5% limits to 'some'.
CF/C23 Percentage of adoptions of looked after children.	Less than 3% limits maximum judgement to 'most'.

Performance Indicator as Key Threshold	Lower Threshold
Adults and Older People	
AO/C26 No. of admissions to residential care for older people per 10,000 pop. AO/C28 No. of households receiving intensive home care (10 hour and six visits a week).	More than 140 per 10,000 pop limits maximum judgement to serving 'some' people well . . . if the C28 is less than 8 per 1000 pop.
AO/C51 No. of Direct Payments	Less than 15 per 100,000 population limits to 'most'.
AO/D54 Percentage of items of community equipment delivered within 7 days.	Less than 45% limits to 'some'. Less than 55% limits to 'most'.
AO/D55 Acceptable waiting times for assessments (percentage of assessments completed within 28 days).	Less than 45% limits to 'some'. Less than 55% limits to 'most'.
AO/D56 Acceptable waiting times for care packages (percentage in place within 28 days of assessment).	Less than 45% limits to 'some'. Less than 55% limits to 'most'.
Ethnicity information – percentage of adult service users assessed or reviewed in the year with ethnic origin not recorded.	More than 15% limits to 'most'.

Figure 7   Key Thresholds and the consequences of not achieving them for 05/06. (CSCI www.csci.org.uk)

PIs are referred to as 'Key Threshold Indicators' (KTs). These KTs have specific performance levels identified below which authorities cannot fall without automatically affecting the overall judgement, and therefore the star rating for the whole CSSR. For some there are two thresholds, falling below the lower threshold limits the CSSR to a maximum judgement that they are only serving 'some' people well. Failure to reach the higher threshold limits the CSSR to the maximum judgement that they are serving 'most' people well. As these 'some' or 'most' judgements are the building blocks of the star rating judgement these KTs could not be more important. The Key Thresholds for 05/06 were as in the table opposite.

The Thresholds set in Figure 7 are not very demanding and not many CSSRs were 'caught' by them in 03/04 or 04/05. However the Thresholds for AO/D54, 55 and 56 were raised 5 per cent for both thresholds for 2004/2005 and have been raised by 5 per cent more for 2005/2006. The impact on a CSSRs star rating if 'caught' by one of the thresholds could be grave. This is a powerful additional control mechanism.

Blobs

The way reported performance is differentiated and published by the CSCI needs a little explanation. When the Audit Commission began publishing the outcomes of the original ACPIs in the 1990s they divided performance of local authorities into 'quartiles'. This is a simple device for dividing the 150 English local authority results for each PI into four groups – with 37 (or 38) authorities in each group. That produced the 'top quartile' – the best performers for that PI – of 37 authorities. The second group were referred to as 'second quartile' performers and so on. This was a purely comparative process with no set standard to aim for. The PAF process, related as it was to national priorities for many of which there were explicit national targets, developed differently. The performance of all 150 authorities against each PI has been reported as being in one of five 'bands'. Where there are numerical targets to reach, performance above the target are placed in the top band. The population of the lower four bandings are decided by a range of means. Where the national targets have been reasonably difficult to reach this is fine as there is a proportionate population of authorities in each band. But for some, where the target has been relatively easy to reach the top band seems over-populated. So in the case of PAF AO/C31 *Adults with a mental health problem helped to live at home per 1000 population aged 18–64* of the 150 English CSSRs no less than 116 were in the top band for 2003/2004, 16 in the second one, 10 in the third and 7 in the fourth. No authority was in the bottom band.

Particular descriptions are used by the CSCI for performance within each of these bands. The top one is always 'very good', the second, 'good' the third 'acceptable', the fourth 'ask questions about performance' and the fifth 'investigate urgently'. The bands are also expressed in the published version in blocks of colour. 'Very good' performance is reported in a rich green. A lighter green means 'good'. Then comes a flat yellow for 'acceptable', then a sort of beige and finally the worst performance, 'investigate urgently' is a hellish red. There is a document published annually which reports the performance of all CSSRs. For each PI there is a table, precisely like a football league table, with the best performance sitting at the top and so on down. This Social Services Performance Assessment Framework Indicators (ibid.) document also shows which band the CSSRs are in for each PI using one, two, three, four or five solid black circles to show which band of performance each CSSR has achieved for each PI. These are universally known as 'blobs' and the report is known as the 'blob' book. Not elegant, but expressive. It demonstrates a perverse affection, I think, for the whole process which belies the constant critical tone of much of the debate. This graphically clear means of representing performance is an additional spur to Directors to 'get those PIs up'. Any 'Investigate urgently' performance with it's livid red and single blob cries out to be sorted out. Unlike many government documents this is a presentational triumph.

Targets and priorities

I have mentioned national targets on several occasions. These are not the only sorts of targets CSSRs have to manage. Each year each CSSR is required to identify an annual target for each of the PAF PIs and other indicators in the Self Assessment documents (DIS for adults and APA for children). These are expected to be 'challenging' but 'realistic'. Generally they have to be made available to the CSCI by the end of May for the forthcoming year. The CSCI Business Relationship Managers make great play of whether the target has been reached or not and the future 'trajectory' of performance predicted. Target setting, was initially, it must be said, crude. Managers may not have paid that much attention to the detail of the definitions, did not really trust data collection methods, had less of a grasp on the processes required to achieve the target and did not have much previous performance data to call on. As the PAF has been in operation since 1998 each council has the benefit of past trends in their performance to inform the discussion about targets. So councils have become more literate targets setters, carefully analysing trends and setting difficult targets where they are expending effort anyway. So the simple expedient of setting as the target a performance which comes just inside the next PI band above previous performance is now widespread. Appropriate effort then has to be made to achieve that target. Although authorities will have different internal priorities no authority can put maximum effort into all aspects of performance. Thus the most important targets and the most effort has generally gone into getting performance out of the lowest bandings – especially the angry red of the 'Investigate Urgently', band.

What has always been unclear is the CSCI response to missed targets. Of the twin exhortations that targets should be both realistic and challenging, which takes precedence? Targets cannot be both realistic, (in which case all should be met), and challenging (in which case some won't).

More problems with PIs

There are a number of common criticisms of PIs. The first, especially from front line staff, is that they are crude. It is suggested that they measure simple activity and have no bearing on the true emotional content of the work or outcomes for service users. But what the PAF PIs set out to measure is in fact a relatively sophisticated set of activities. I believe the general perception of crudity is for three interconnected reasons; over ambition in creating the PIs, managers in CSSRs interpreting PI definitions in the simplest way and PIs which (because they do not quite cover the appropriate ground required by the objectives) divert attention away from those objectives.

The ambition of the DoH in 1998 may have been commendable, but it has sown some confusion. Alongside straightforward PIs, like CF/C20, *The number of child protection reviews completed on time* and AO/C26 and AO/C27, *The numbers of adults and older people admitted to long term residential care*, much more sophisticated PIs were established, such as CF/A3, *Re-registrations on the Child Protection register* and AO/D42, *The numbers of carers receiving assessments* and AO/C28, *Intensive Home Care*. These require some statistical understanding to interpret. I believe there has been a tendency within CSSRs to incorporate the simplest interpretation of these into the performance debate, and a complementary tendency in the CSCI to press CSSRs on their performance less fully on the more sophisticated measures than with the PIs which seem simpler.

Another problem is that although PIs purport to measure the outcomes of national priorities the power of the individual PI is now so strong that policy direction in some CSSRs is dominated by the PI and not the actual policy. Thus the target to increase the number of adoptions was outlined in *Improvement, Expansion and Reform: The Next Three Years' Priorities and Planning Framework 2003/2006* (see DoH website). But as well as the increases demanded in the actual number of adoptions there are two other aspects to the overall target:

> By 2004/05 the proportion of children placed for adoption within 12 months of the decision that adoption is in the child's bests interests should increase to 95 per cent.

and:

> To maintain current levels of adoption placement stability (as measured by the proportion of placements for adoption ending with the making of an

adoption order) so that the quality is not compromised whilst increasing the use of adoption.

It is the latter point which is interesting, because the concentration is on the stability of the placement before the adoption order is made. Adoption lies at the heart of the policy demanding improved quality of life for Looked After Children, but sensitive as the whole process is, no PI requires a quality check on the increasing numbers of adoptions achieved. There is, for instance, no national requirement to measure the number of adoption breakdowns – only anecdotal evidence that breakdowns are on the increase. This is a clear case of a numerical increase in activity being demanded and the quality of the activity being ignored.

Furthermore common sense assumptions about comparisons between seemingly matched PIs can cause problems. A move away from institutions toward community provision was at the heart of the government's 1998 policy. So would not consideration of two PIs which seem to measure the decrease in residential provision and the increase in community provision provide evidence of what is happening? The two obvious comparators are:

PAF AO/C26, The number of long term residential and nursing home admissions of older people per 10,000 population over 65.

. . . discussed above and:

PAF PI	98/99	99/00	00/01	01/02	02/03	03/04
C26 – The number of older people admitted to long term residential care per 10,000 population over 65.	128.0	125.0	109.0	109.0	101.0	98.0
C26 – numbers of people in the numerator.	99,929	97,587	85,096	85,096	78,850	76,508
C28 – The number of households receiving more than 10 hours domiciliary care and six visits a week per 1000 population.	7.9	8.9	9.3	9.9	10.3	11.1
C28 – numbers of people in the numerator.	61,675	69,482	72,605	77,289	80,412	86,657

Figure 8   Comparison of PI PAF AO/C26 and PAF PI AO/C28 (Population figures are extrapolated from the reported PIs using 2001 census figures)

*PAF AO/C28, the number of households in receipt of intensive home care (more than 10 hours home care **and** six visits by a home carer) per 10,000 of the population over 65.*

If the policy of de-institutionalisation is working then those people who might previously have been admitted to residential care will be those supported with over ten hours home care with more than six visits a week. Indeed one of the Key Thresholds for adults included in Figure 7 explicitly links the two PIs in a joint threshold.

The comparative figures over a six year period demonstrate an impressive correlation between reducing admissions and increasing intensive home care. Unfortunately the correlation is more apparent than real. The populations measured by AO/C26 and AO/C28 are not equivalent. There are a number of differences:

- AO/C26 includes nursing home admissions, people who have complex nursing needs who would be very difficult to care for at home for any length of time,
- AO/C26 only includes those people who are assessed as falling below the financial threshold and therefore does not include people not funded by CSSRs. Some people above the financial threshold for home care still choose to receive home care via social services.
- People receiving the amount of care which makes them eligible for AO/C28 but who receive a Direct Payment cannot be counted in AO/C28.
- The biggest discrepancy is, however, that in AO/C26 only older people admitted to residential care are counted. In the numerator for AO/C28 all **households** receiving ten hours care and six visits a week are counted. This, in an average CSSR, would consist of a majority services users over 65, but might include anything between 15 per cent and 30 per cent of younger disabled people. The denominator for C28 is the population of older people, giving the impression to someone casually scrutinising this PI that it is all about older people. It is not, it is about the whole population over 18.

Despite these discrepancies the CSCI look at these two PIs as if they were in direct correlation. So they are included in consideration about the judgement for the star rating, even though for most CSSRs the comparison of the data from these PIs is useless as any sort of guide for future policy development or operational practice.

More than this AO/C28 may actually be dangerous for the future care of vulnerable adults and older people. The pressure has been unremitting in achieving an increase in the AO/C28 'score'. This has not just meant that social workers have been expected to commission eleven hours care, when nine would do, but militates against a proper review of the care commissioned. As the increase in AO/C28 is such a high profile requirement, when a review is undertaken reductions in packages below the ten hour threshold become problematic for social workers to propose. No allowance either has been made in the PI for the frail and vulnerable person receiving an intensive package growing in confidence or capacity to cope. It may be that the package recipient may, in the fullness of time, no longer need more than ten hours care, but no data collection about that phenomenon is required. The policy objective is 'independence' of vulnerable people, but the pressure to improve performance against PI AO/C28 may be delivering dependence at home rather than dependence in residential care. This problem is recognised by the CSCI and AO/C28 will, I am sure, soon be amended.

Another problem occurs when PIs are used as a sort of policy bludgeon. This is happening with PI AO/C51, Direct Payments. The ministers responsible have continued to demand breakneck increases in the numbers of Direct Payments offered to people with disabilities (Ladyman, 2005). The Direct Payments PI is now a Key Threshold, signifying the very highest profile for this activity. No one can argue that Direct Payments are not consistent with the general direction of the policy to offer service users more autonomy and independence. But the number of Direct Payments has been doubling each year anyway and the demands made by government might turn a wonderful policy into a blind juggernaut. Not all people are the same and not all services suit all people. Situations where implementation of the policy becomes a more pressing driver than individual people's needs are potentially dangerous. That way lie future disasters comparable with the expansion of residential care for older people in the 1980s, which was done in the name of choice.

There is another subtle problem. The PAF data set is dominated by PIs which relate to the national objectives, the most pressing in 1998 being seen as:

- Establishing more independent forms of care for older people.
- Testing the robustness of child protection procedures.
- Confirming quality of life for Looked After Children.

The assessment processes also attracted a number of PIs. There were also generic PIs for adults and older people but adult service user groups other than older people were otherwise ignored. Also ignored were services directed at children in need, almost all direct provision (save that for Looked After Children), prevention work for both adults and children, human resource issues, most of training, IT and planning. As Pearce and King point out lots of PIs for children's services were established which tested efficiency, but fewer tested economy or effectiveness (Pearce and King, 2004). John Dixon commented in 2005 that the PAF PI set 'tend to drive activity in the direction of the ideals of a decade ago and in some instances . . . away from current aspirations' (Dixon, 2005). And David Johnstone, Director of Devon Social Services and chair of the Standards and Performance Committee of the ADSS, observed that 'at the moment . . . the emphasis of performance assessment in social care is around higher level, institutional based care' (Samuel, 2005).

Thus the PAF has established an emphasis on specific service user groups, intensive intervention and certain processes. Equally this has meant that some services have been hidden away from the heightened profile PAF PIs bestow. This has wide ramifications. For instance the speedy computerisation of CSSR activity over the last several years has been fastest in those areas where PAF PIs demand activity. There is therefore greater IT literacy amongst field social workers than other staff, greater access to IT training and equipment and much greater involvement in IT application development. We'll consider the impact of this in the next chapter.

Gaming and resistance

In their survey of the revival in local government in the US written in the early 1990s Osbourne and Gaebler quote James Q. Wilson in his description of an archetypal example of 'gaming' with performance measurement (Osborne and Gaebler, 1992). Under pressure in the late 1970s to produce evidence that they were achieving ever increasing numbers of arrests Wilson says of the FBI in the US:

> To meet their goals, they began to ask local police departments for lists of stolen cars that had been found – so they could claim them as recoveries. To increase the numbers of fugitives apprehended, they began concentrating on military deserters, who were far easier to find than normal criminals. By the late 1970s US attorneys were declining to prosecute 60 per cent of the cases the FBI presented, often because they were so trivial.

While not as spectacular as this example the reader will have noticed in this text several examples of 'gaming' to meet targets already; the temptation to close down initial assessments for children before the work is complete, the temptation to commission ten hours home care for disabled people even if they do not need it, the temptation of not recording the actual number of admissions of older people to residential care. The reader will no doubt be able to pinpoint others. As we saw in Chapter 2 there are a number of pitfalls and temptations in the use of PIs, most of which redirect attention from the service to the management of the PI itself. That's what gaming is. Although 'gaming' is a feature of all organisational life and not just performance measurement processes, general knowledge across the organisation that performance indicators can be manipulated is a comfort to those who are resistant to the introduction of such disciplines. Gaming, ill focussed PIs and oppressive demands from above to focus on the PIs easily lead to dismissal of performance measurement arrangements, especially in the current cultural context where the public perception of 'targets' is so negative.

Resistance to the use of performance indicators, for whatever reason, is a regular occurrence in public service organisations where they are introduced. Osbourne and Gaebler suggest that the pattern of early resistance to performance measurement in local government, and the use of PIs in particular, is general:

> *This pattern – adoption of crude performance measures, followed by protest and pressure to improve measures, followed by the development of more sophisticated measures is common wherever performance is measured.*
>
> Osborne and Gaebler, op. cit.

Resistance has been played out within CSSRs between different groups of managers, especially front line staff and organisation leaders. But even some senior managers have sometimes attempted to hide from the pressures imposed by the PAF. In my experience the responses of less engaged operational managers to those collating the PAF data has developed along the following lines:

> *1998/1999 – 'This PAF and these PIs haven't got anything to do with us have they? Just get on with it will you'*
>
> *1999/2000 – 'I can't quite see the point of all this. That data system's not reliable is it?'*
>
> *2000/2001 – 'We dispute those figures of yours. Yes I know they are entered by our staff but they're not right'.*
>
> *2001/2002 –'Why aren't we doing better than this? Can't we report these amended figures just this once to make the return reflect what actually happens?'*
>
> *2002/2003 – 'What do we have to change to report accurately what is going on?'*
>
> *2003/2004 – 'OK, these figures look better now we've sorted out our processes – but do they really tell us anything?'*

But for such managers there is no escape. The world has changed. Previously the big drivers of policy were major changes in legislation or practice initiatives such as the introduction of the 'Orange Book' guidance. Similarly a lot of research was sponsored previously by the DoH. This has now retreated to universities. There was also in the past much more scope for local discretion in prioritising activity and policy making. In many ways the traditional manner of operation of social care in Britain until the mid 1990s was comparable to a loosely linked set of craft organisations. Despite various attempts to impose national standards there were variations in practice and expectation across the country. Some CSSRs admitted a lot of older people to residential care, some relatively few; some had strings of children's homes, some none; some dealt with applicants quickly, others with laxity. Cultures of good practice and acceptable services differed from team to team. Not any more. There are variations in practice, but not in expectation; not in management objectives. Associated with that transformation of social care from a craft to a national industry is a revolution in the day to day work of social work and social care staff, particularly those working in field teams. This has largely been brought about by performance measurement requirements, more stringent recording requirements and the comprehensive introduction of IT applications at the core of the work. What social care staff actually spend their time doing and the way they approach it is completely different from ten years ago. Unfortunately for these teams, and there are thousands of workers involved, no one not working on the front line appears to have noticed.

Summary

The performance measurement process for social care developed by central government is an integrated process, identifying national priorities, (linked, notionally at least, with NHS priorities), specific objectives and timetabled targets. Associated with this have been targeted grants. Linked with this strategic thrust are a range of Performance Indicators (including 50 high level ones, the PAF set) which are reported every year and contribute to an assessment of the achievements and potential of both adult social care and the social care aspects of children's services. The PAF set of PIs are the most high profile aspect of this network of processes on the front line. Some are focussed. Others have confused staff and managers and some have, it is thought, helped to direct activity away from the real priorities. The interpretation of some PIs is sometimes less straightforward than the definitions imply. This is compounded by the several slight mismatches between PIs and the policy objectives, and the confusion and misdirected effort that entails. The PAF PIs reflect the priorities of the late 1990s. It is also arguable that it is not any crudeness of PIs which is the major problem, but rather the ambitions of the system – a system trying to do too much too quickly. There have been a variety of responses to the introduction of this process and an impact on priorities, practice and organisational direction which we shall attempt to analyse in the next chapter.

Exercise 1

Osbourne and Gaebler have considered in detail the case made against introducing performance measurement arrangements into public services.

They have offered a set of aphorisms to convince public service managers of the dangers of not taking this approach to their business. There are seven:

1. What gets measured gets done.
2. If you don't measure results you cannot tell success from failure.
3. If you can't see success you can't reward it.
4. If you can't reward success you're probably rewarding failure.
5. If you can't see success you can't learn from it.
6. If you can't recognise failure you can't correct it.
7. If you can demonstrate results you can win public support.

Osborne and Gaebler, op. cit.

So much quoted are these phrases they fall into the category of organisational cliché. Nevertheless these comments are worth considering – whether you think they represent the fundamentals of performance measurement or glib management speak. Debate within your team what they mean to you. Such discussion might clarify the understanding of such words as **result**, **success**, **failure**, reward and '**public support**'.

Exercise 2

Ask your manager to see the 'Blob' book (CSCI, 2005a) and the Annual Performance Assessment Self Assessment (for children's social care) or for adult social care the DIS. See how long it takes to track them down.

Look at the PIs in the Blob book and work out how many your team or unit has responsibility for. Make a list of them. For each PI:

- Check how your organisation is doing.
- How is your team doing? Is performance broken down by your department and available for you to see at team level?
- Do you know what you should be doing to improve your performance for each PI?
- Does that requirement make sense in operational terms? Does it help the service user?
- Could you improve on how you are expected to act to improve the PI?

Finally work out if there is any training or support you and your colleagues might need to help you become more effective.

Chapter 4

Analysis

Four Questions

In previous chapters I have discussed the details of the system and set out the stated purposes of the various aspects of it. In this chapter I take a broader view of the underlying principles and implications of the process. This analysis concentrates on four questions:

1. What is the philosophy behind the system and what are its intentions?
2. Does the system work? Is it, to borrow a phrase, serving people well?
3. What are the implications and consequences of the system?

The fourth question, 'How could it be improved?' will be considered in the next chapter.

Philosophy and intentions

The overriding social care policy goal since 1998 has been to help vulnerable citizens to retain, regain or improve their ability to live safely and independently. The policy is at root anti-institutional and socially inclusive, a more focussed continuation of the community care thrust of the previous thirty years. But each of the three New Labour administrations have had a slightly different emphasis.

The stated ideology in the first term was decidedly unideological. It was exemplified by the, at the time, oft quoted desire to act in a 'third way', neither favouring private sector provision nor the earlier orthodoxy that public servants are the only group that can serve the public. There have been politically charged debates about the long term efficacy of using the Private Finance Initiative to lever in capital for large scale building programmes, but broad sympathy within the social care world for the overall aim. And in the first term the policy thrust was almost indistinguishable from that of NHS; to provide more good services for more people more efficiently. This explains the concentration in the PAF data set in 'collecting' more service users; undertaking more reviews, completing more processes to timescales. Initially the traditional social care services focus on the most vulnerable and poor people at times of crisis was retained, explaining the emphasis in the PAF set on high intervention services.

These policy goals developed in New Labour's second term. The concentration was on ways of breaking down the walls between different organisations and establishing better partnerships between health, public protection and social care organisations. The need for more services remained paramount, with more of an emphasis on making the 'whole system' serve the individual's needs. But the general thrust remained both utilitarian and directed at those in greatest need.

However if the underlying philosophy was utilitarian from 1998, there are now libertarian tinges appearing in the 'outcome' focus being discussed during Blair's third term. If 'efficiency' characterised the policy thrust of the 1980s and 'assessment' the 1990s, 'outcomes' is the word which most completely sums up the aspiration of the government for social care in the first decade of the twenty first century. Very similar approaches have been adopted for the children's services assessment programme as those signposted by the Adult Services Green Paper, *Independence, Wellbeing and Choice* and the Health and Social Care White Paper published in early 2006.

The government seems to be attempting to shift the local authority response to citizens' needs in three directions. Firstly is the aspiration to leave behind the traditional welfare rationing approach and offer more low level direct services, more quickly to more people. Secondly is the desire to offer a more completely responsive and tailored service to those with more pressing and complex needs. Thirdly is the requirement that social care become part of the mainstream council response to citizens' needs rather than remaining a rather embarrassing sideshow for the poor. Use of such language as service users being 'In Control', and 'Self Assessment' signals a shift towards viewing the individual citizen as negotiator rather than simple recipient.

This raises questions about the future of the traditional pattern of work in social care: the assessment, care plan and service delivery cycle. It also rests uneasily with the public protection aspects of social care. There are also questions about the financial sustainability of such an approach in the face of the increasing numbers of older people, increasing fragmentation of family life and increasing public expectations. But it chimes in perfectly with the modernisation thrust discussed below.

The mechanism for delivering the policy of improvement in social care has been simple behaviourism. The original stimulus for CSSRs was the considerable funding made available from 1998 to deliver precisely identified objectives. From 2002 this has been supplemented by the threat of a damning judgement about the CSSR. This elicits the response of directing effort to avoid criticism in the annual performance cycle. This mechanism, which has been extraordinarily effective, has been reached, in my view, by chance. Had the process been introduced in one go it would not have taken hold – too much all at once to incorporate into an organisation's culture. Acceptance has been secured by the staggered introduction of different aspects of it; the slow accretion since 1993 of relevant PIs, individual investigation of the whole CSSRs in Joint Reviews, the identification then of national objectives and standards, the introduction of the PAF in 1998 and finally public judgements with real consequences based on annual assessments in 2002. Joint Reviews were introduced in an attempt to create a comprehensive judgement about CSSRs in 1996. When the PAF was introduced in 1998 it was not comprehensively incorporated into the Joint Review process. Thus a four year period of acclimatisation was created for the PAF before the results of it were used in earnest. The masterstroke was the shift from reliance on the infrequent sledgehammer of the Joint Review to the steady drip, drip of the annual assessment process in 2002. That the DoH stumbled upon this process rather than launched it as part of a grand plan is a tribute to the flexibility and persistence of those concerned.

A consequence of this slowly assembled 'carrot and stick' is the 'buy in' which has been achieved amongst senior and middle managers in social services. People obliged to undertake certain actions in the face of unpleasant consequences for non-compliance tend to be open to the philosophical justifications for these actions. When they become used to them, they are more likely to champion the underlying ideas than before they were forced to act in that way. Driving etiquette is an example of this phenomenon. Drink driving and not wearing a seat belt only became socially unacceptable once people were obliged, by law, to belt up and not drink. The 'mindset', follows the actions in self justification. This works for managers close enough to the leadership of the organisation to share the fear of the negative consequences of a low star rating.

Another philosophical underpinning of the performance assessment cycle is the notion of 'modernisation' demanded by the New Labour administrations since 1997. At first the administration underestimated the difficulties of modernising public services. Tony Blair's 'scars on my back' aside in 2002 relating to the difficulties he had in convincing senior civil servants of the need to modernise public services could just as well have been made about local government . Modernisation of public services for New Labour seems to have several intricately related features:

- Joined up thinking between different public services.
- Greater openness and accountability.
- Use of IT to the maximum benefit of the citizen.
- Using the latest business practices to establish efficient, dependable services with consistent and rising standards, i.e. what works is what matters.

- Meeting the expectations of citizens by treating them as customers, much as commercial organisations do.

This view of modernisation should not be confused with the ideological determination of the Thatcher governments to have public services operate as businesses. This government only requires the comprehensive use of business disciplines. One of the major drivers of modernisation is severely practical. During the early and mid 1990s while local authorities were still relying on creaking mainframes for their IT services many commercial organisations had jumped on the potential of the internet and developed expertise in 24 availability, interactive web sites, call centres and so on. It is clear, just from glancing at the government's e-govt strategy, that the administration's vision is for each public service to take full advantage of these facilities, so that all are operating as a sort of Amazon.gov.uk by the end of 2005. The origins of the expectation that all local government services will be available electronically can be found in the White Paper *Modernising Government*. March 1999. (Cm 4310.)

But this means that local authorities have had to change the way they relate to the public, offering evening and weekend availability, immediate information and quick decisions. This in itself implies a 'commodification' of local authority services, social care included. I use this mouthful of a word because it is the clearest I can think of. It means that local authority services, including social care services, are deliberately turned into commodities. There are two reasons for attempting this. First of all this approach can reduce the stigma associated with using social care services (and the lower level stigma associated with 'council' services). This can be done by blurring the boundary between seeking help from social services and, say, renewing your car insurance. If the process becomes indistinguishable it is less likely, the argument goes, that people will shy away from approaching CSSRs. This is a key driver behind the establishment of contact centres for social care services. A nice example of where this has already been achieved is around the issue of Blue Parking Badges. Not so long ago Blue Badges were only made available to people after a personal interview and 'assessment'. In many local authorities these are now available once an applicant has completed an electronic form on the web site. The criteria, nationally set, have not changed, but the protective, 'professional' attitude towards the availability of this benefit has disappeared.

The other reason for taking this commodification approach is that it is what people expect in every other sphere of their lives. They can conduct a great deal of their personal business over the phone at all times of the day or night or on the internet. Why not social care? People want services to be accessible, timely, seamless, delivered with courtesy and effectiveness. This approach speaks to the huge majority of people who contact social care organisations who do so to ask about the availability of child minders, how to get community meals for their mother, Blue Badges and other simple things. The underlying belief here is that if organisational processes are completed properly then people will be served. Does this undermine social work practice? Does it endanger people who really should be given a more comprehensive and personal response? Whatever the result of any debate it is the case now that social care services no longer sit in a quiet corner reacting to requests from those brave or unfortunate enough to come to their attention, but are in the full glare of public expectation and the government's ambition to improve services for citizens.

Does the system serve people well?

We have to break this question down. There are several constituencies interested in the results of the system; the government, social services authorities and senior managers, front line staff and managers, service users and the general public. But before approaching this question we should consider whether across the whole of commerce and public service performance measurement offers real benefits to organisations which adopt it.

There is a considerable literature about performance measurement and the use of such tools as balanced scorecards, but most of it is explanation and exhortation. What there is on the effectiveness of performance measurement offers a broad consensus of opinion (see Bourne et al., 2000). In general terms performance measurement systems are seen to provide a positive structure which supports the improvement of an organisation's performance. But some organisations introduce performance measurement more successfully than others. Lingle and Schiemann suggest that those companies with performance measurement systems which offer clear benefits are characterised by:

- General agreement amongst managers on the strategy.
- Clear communication across the organisation.
- Alignment of effort and focus on what matters.
- A positive culture.

Lingle and Schiemann, 1996.

Neely and his colleagues have done considerable work on performance measurement and in linked papers in 2002 and 2003 investigated the characteristics of successful implementation of performance measurement systems. They concluded that:

Many of the issues raised in implementation were connected with change management issues ... the application of the process and the content of the resulting performance measurement system were not major factors in determining the success or failure of implementations, while softer contextual factors such as 'purpose' and 'management commitment' were.

Bourne et al., 2003.

Neely et al., in an earlier case study, concluded that there were three major obstacles to the introduction of performance measurement systems:

1. Resistance to measurement.
2. Computer systems issues.
3. Top management commitment being distracted.

Bourne et al., 2000.

Similarly de Waal stresses the importance of 'soft' issues:

Performance measurement and control systems cannot be designed without taking into account human behaviour . . . Positive outcomes are generated by better strategic alignment of employees and better motivation, which indicates that causal relationships exist between performance management system design, management control use, managerial and employee behaviour and performance.

De Waal, 2003.

So performance measurement processes offer benefits, but more so if the implementation takes account of organisational culture and the human aspects of the organisation. It is worth noting that all the academic studies mentioned here looked at systems which were developed and implemented by organisations themselves, not imposed by an external body as the social care system has been.

Back to social care. Does the system serve people well? We'll start with **the government**. The answer in three ways is a resounding yes. First of all everybody, the social services in all 150 English local authorities, plays the game. The consequences of not joining in are too grave to contemplate as reputation and direction would be in jeopardy, partner organisations would look askance and the recalcitrance of the CSSR would soon be the stuff of editorials in the local press. The development of the mechanism is a stunning success for government which in one way or another has been trying to achieve this sort of control for a generation.

Secondly the government knows much more about social services than it has before; numbers, timeliness, attitudes, patterns. Notwithstanding failings in the quality of some of the data and the difficulty in interpreting a lot of it, this is a policy maker's dream. And as an increasing amount of the PAF data in particular is drawn directly from the databases used for recording work with individual service users it is more comprehensive, detailed and accurate than anything available from NHS services. There is of course a caution here about the potential misuse or misunderstanding of intelligence. Ministers and senior officials in the DfES and DoH may have considerable amounts of data

PAF PI	98/99	99/00	00/01	01/02	02/03	03/04	04/05
CF/C22 – Children under 10 looked after in foster care or placed for adoption (as opposed to residential care).	81%	82%	83%	96%	97%	98%	98%
CF/C23 – Adoptions of Children Looked After within the year.	4%	4.7%	5.2%	6.8%	6.9%	7.5%	7.6%
AO/D39 – Adult service users receiving a statement of their needs and how they will be met (i.e. a care plan).	N/A	78%	81%	84%	86%	89%	91%
AO/D40 – Adult service users receiving a review.	N/A	N/A	42%	47%	51%	59%	63%

Figure 9   Significant Improvements in PAF PIs since its introduction. (England averages from Social Services PAF Indicators, Nov 2004, CSCI, www.csci.org.uk) (some of the increases have benefited from definition changes over the years).

and they might confuse that with knowing what it means. As Pearce and King point out:

> For most PIs . . . national data collections do not yet adequately align linkages between measures of activity, expenditure, staffing and outcome which would make [a] fuller assessment possible.
>
> Pearce and King, 2004.

Thirdly and most impressively the improvement in reported performance against some of the measures identified has been startling. Again, leave aside for a moment criticism about data quality, gaming and the questionable focus of some of the PIs. Just consider the reported improvements over a six year period in Figure 9.

Much of this book rehearses a range of criticisms about the performance measurement and assessment process, but this cannot just be the story of the problems of the system because in large measure it is delivering what it is intended to.

In large measure the system is delivering what it is intended to . . . within its own terms. And those terms are narrowly focussed. For instance the PIs which measure the educational attainment of Looked After Children require extra effort to go into educating the most deprived group of young people in the country. But the process has little impact on the longer term inclusion or life chances of such children. Similarly the increase in the number of disabled people being 'helped to live at home' means nothing if they can never go out into the world without being stared at or thwarted by incomprehensible bus timetables. The successes reported above cannot be dismissed as mere statistics but are of single aspects of services – narrow proxies at most for quality of life or independence. They are not evidence of broad lifestyle advances for vulnerable people.

There is also the danger that government agencies believe in the success of the system more than other stakeholders. The following statement comes from a joint report from the Audit Commission and the IDeA about a conference hosted under the Performance Management, Measurement and Information (PMMI) project:

> . . . *the Comprehensive Performance Assessment [process] demonstrate[s] that performance management is a key characteristic in the success of a well run local authority.*

See IDEA, 2005.

This is true, but is a tautology. The AC has imposed a performance measurement process on councils and then judged them against it. But the proposition that councils are offering services which citizens believe to be better is unproven.

Indeed one of the government's problems is that the **general public** still has to be convinced about it. Despite the efforts made over the last years the only national measure of satisfaction with local government as a whole shows an embarrassing decline. The 2004 survey of general satisfaction conducted by all councils reported a 10 per cent reduction in overall satisfaction with services compared to the equivalent survey undertaken in 2001. This does not focus on social care and the outcome could be interpreted in a range of ways but it is not good news (ODPM, 2004). In social care one of the difficult selling points with a policy thrust based on independence and helping people stay in their own homes is that public events are more likely to be the closure of facilities; residential homes and day care facilities for instance, compared to the opening of brand new buildings of which the NHS can always boast. We also know that even if a citizen's personal experience of social care (or any public service) is good, they are still likely to take a pessimistic view of the quality or availability of services nationally. I had a conversation with my grown up daughter which exemplifies this problem. Sophie has 'green' views and was trying to convince me that the three coloured plastic bins we had just received from the council were worth the effort of filling to recycle more waste material. After I grumpily accepted her logic she commented dismissively of the council's motivation that they were 'only doing it to meet their recycling targets', as if that were a shameful motivation. This dissonance between the understanding that many council policies are worthwhile and the view that councils should first and always be understood to have base motivations is, I believe, widespread.

The picture is similar for **service users**. The improved performance reported against a range of PIs would indicate that service users have benefited from performance processes. But the PIs concentrate on service delivered, timeliness or processes. They do not record the reaction of the recipients. Increasingly satisfaction surveys are a part of the PAF process – all of which over the last few years indicate an improvement in reported satisfaction and responsiveness. There is no reason not to take these findings at face value. But the focus of these surveys has been exclusively on what services are offered. No attention has been paid to alternatives the service user might have preferred. Thus until the mid 1990s cleaning was commissioned on a regular basis for older people with low level needs. The beneficiaries might have reported satisfaction with what they regarded as a very good service. Such people do not receive any such service now and are not asked whether they might like to because no CSSR can afford it. And people admitted to residential care may report that they are content, but have had no means of suggesting that they would have preferred to stay at home.

The major problem here is that there have been no attempts to collate the overall service user experience and no concerted attempt to seek comment from 'outside' the system. Even general citizen surveys conducted across whole local authorities tend to ask how satisfied people are with social services. No one is asked whether they wanted to contact social services in the first place.

The formal surveys required by the PAF are mostly administered 'cold', by letter rather than face to face. And the service users asked may feel they have a vested interest in answering positively . . . just in case. There is also no benchmark data; no comparison available from before the PAF and its pressures was introduced. I am inclined to believe that most service users are better off than five years ago, but cannot find real evidence for this. On the other hand there are numerous examples, as we saw in chapter one, of individuals discomfited by the power of the PAF PI.

For **social services authorities** the answer to the 'serving well' question has to be yes and no. There is a clarity and precision about what senior managers have to achieve that is still relatively new in social services, and an urgency that can be exhilarating. Councillors may feel surplus to requirements as the policy direction is all centrally driven and Pinkney suggests the central focus of performance assessment arrangements runs counter to the other policy drivers which laud localisation, devolution and flexibility (Pinkney, 1998).

The focus of activity has sharpened considerably. What staff have to do, and what their team's work is judged against is more clear cut. Energy to improve certain aspects of work is more directed. The outputs of the organisations are better known and available to all. There have also been considerable shifts in the way some of the work is undertaken, whether it is the predictability of child protection reviews, the timeliness of the delivery of community equipment, the number of children looked after in homely settings or the numbers of admissions of older people to residential care. As Pearce and King observe the process has 'shined a light into some dark places . . . foregrounding' as they put it, some previously hidden activities (Pearce and King, op. cit.).

But the performance assessment process is hungry. The CSCI suggest that performance against PIs should be treated as the beginning of the assessment conversation rather than the totality. It is also suggested that preparations for the annual assessment process should not create work additional to that required by the annual planning cycle. As Miller suggests 'whether or not the [CSCI's] apparent minimal reliance on PIs is to be believed, there is no doubt that other stakeholders do take the PI scores . . . extremely seriously' (Miller, op. cit.). I doubt if there is a director or senior social care manager in the land who acts otherwise. Considerable organisation and effort is required to feed this machine. In addition the pressures of the system lead some CSSRs to set targets which are more ambitious than their capacity to deliver. The CSCI may be happy with that seductive ambition, 'and the CSSR will appear to be more 'successful'. But 'if', as Miller says 'the out-turn data reveal the . . . target to have been unrealistic the reverse applies . . . the star rating regime may deliver better performance but it has an in-built tendency to lead also to economy with the truth in self reporting' (ibid.). Finally it is worth quoting Miller again summing up the impact on CSSRs.

> *Much is changing and changing for the better – though it would be difficult to assess at what cost in financial terms and in terms of morale of front line staff'.*

ibid.

So for **operational staff and first line managers** the picture, as we noted in the first chapter, is not entirely positive. Tony Hunter, ADSS president in 2005, says, 'the star rating system [has] brought senior managers and front line staff together by forcing directors to concentrate on the right things by making directors accountable'. But this is too rosy a view. There is anecdotal evidence of senior managers demanding of junior managers (and so on down the line) that performance against particular PIs has to be improved come what may. This Leaden Threat in place of the Golden Thread is hardly likely to enamour staff of the processes that result in such pressure. Pearce and King, writing in 2003, concluded:

> *Overall social workers, even in the most PI aware authority, seem far from engaged with the performance agenda . . . The notion that some PIs might*

lead to improved outcomes is readily accepted, but doubts about their validity is greatest here.

Pearce and King, op. cit.

I have searched the performance management guidelines of the DoH, DfES, the AC and CSCI for comments about the role of staff working face to face with service users but there is little. Advice and expectations are offered to councillors and managers, but not specifically to staff. Thus the helpful IDeA booklet Making Performance Management Work; a practical guide (see IDeA website) gives advice about the CPA and corporate performance management to councillors and senior managers but not line managers. It is as if front line staff have no role.

But there is some help. In November 2004 the West Midlands ADSS in concert with Tribal/SECTA, a consultancy firm, published a guide for front line social services managers on 'the connections between daily tasks and corporate objectives and to gain and promote the ownership of performance data' (see West Midlands ADSS, 2005). The guidebook lays out a model workshop designed to engage first line managers in debate about the intricacies of performance measurement. The starting point is revealing. The advice for those running workshops is unequivocal. 'Be aware that people will want to pick holes in the performance indicators required by central government and use the arguments described [in an earlier section of the guide] to explain why they are not an accurate reflection of the work that they do'. And 'encourage people to channel their dislike of central government statistics into the creation of new measures . . . emphasise that whilst local performance indicators will add great value at local level, the central government offices will still expect their statutory returns, performance indicators etc'. And finally the guide demands that the workshop leader allows 'time for an outpouring of negative comments'.

So the expectation that front line staff will revile the performance indicators and everything associated with them seems to be widespread. An anonymous letter in Community Care in 2005 encapsulates this:

> . . . *directors take note and reflect that for authorities with the top rating the amount of additional paperwork to support performance targets to maintain a three-star rating adds to caseload pressures without any tangible benefits for front line staff.*

Community Care, 2005.

This conforms to the analysis that the real work goes on at the front line despite the machinations of managers. Such criticism can be dismissed as relatively unsophisticated but it is widespread. Introducing managerial ideas to front line staff has inherent difficulties. Take the idea of business planning – an integral part of the performance process, and firmly urged on local authorities by the CSCI. Business planning disciplines are clear and understandable to service managers, or for team managers with new structures or services to introduce. But for staff on the front line – where the pattern of work coming their way does not change much from one year to the next – there is a difficulty. More staff or the increasing availability of alternative services are welcome but business planning cannot be central to the work of front line staff. That's for the senior people, runs the argument. 'It doesn't affect us, we get on with stuff day by day'. So 'selling' business planning (and by implication performance measurement) to front line units is problematic.

The work done also presents problems. Froggatt suggests that 'technical rational' approaches to performance measurement conflict with what front line staff deal with, 'intractable disorganisation and irrationality', which makes staff less likely to take the 'technical rational' seriously (Froggatt, 2002). Furthermore successes in the front line have not, generally, been celebrated other than within the local team and have not lent themselves to being collated. So local evidence of good 'performance', whether complementing or confronting PI performance is limited. Furthermore the human achieve-ments of CSSRs are often less concrete than those in other public services. We have nothing so clear cut as exam results, offender reconviction rates or ambulance response rates. Raine and Willson speak of a 'disconnection between the view of performance . . . managers . . . see in their PIs – of disappointing standards and inefficiency . . . and the viewpoint of . . . staff who may . . . perceive themselves to be working diligently and effectively . . .'(Raine and Willson, 1997). All this has added to the difficulties the CSCI have had in introducing performance measurement.

However, underpinning all these concerns is, as Miller says, 'a perception of mistrust'.

> *The PI regime is perceived to be predicated on a belief that workers will not be doing their best for users and carers and the need to be coerced to do so by measurement and reporting . . . the removal of discretion and judgement in a sphere of work which is of its very nature responsive and diverse is demotivating.*

Miller, op. cit.

The involvement and response of one other community deserves some comment – that of social work educators and academics, who seem oblivious to all of this. For instance *Social Work Futures: Crossing Boundaries, Transforming Practice*, published in 2005, contains 21 essays about the full range of social work practice and processes and purports to offer discussion of the concerns of the whole social work and social care community. Only one of these essays makes any comment about the performance assessment process; that entitled 'Review' by Lorna Ball and even the comment there is in passing.

I am not suggesting for one moment that the performance assessment process and PIs should be regarded as at the heart of practice development. But the performance assessment regime impinges upon how policy develops within the CSSR, the practice of all front line staff, supervision, quality audit programmes and so on. But most of all the demands of the PIs and case recording systems, as we shall see, dominate the social worker's day to day working life. The potential crossover between the performance assessment processes, evaluation tools and research activity is considerable. But none of this stuff, eight years after its introduction, appears to be on the social work educator's radar.

If the roles of educators and academics are to educate social workers and social care workers and to contribute to the development of practice through research and debate, then in both these roles, in this severely practical matter, the social work education community is failing dismally.

Conclusion

The impact of both the broad disciplines and the detailed processes has been a mixed bag. There is evidence that where PIs are clear, and funding to back up the target has been available, considerable change in service users' lives has resulted. The stronger impact of the system has been to guarantee that CSSRs follow national policy direction rather than to respond to the needs of local people. This may seem a cruel comment, but for CSSRs the CSCI is a more insistent 'customer' than the father ringing up asking for help looking after his disabled child.

Finally, the imposition of performance measurement from outside CSSRs has caused considerable problems. As is implied by the brief review of performance measurement literature above, successful implementation is seen to rely on taking the human and cultural aspects of the organisation seriously enough to involve staff and managers up and down the line. Sterling efforts have been made in many CSSRs to do this, but senior managers are starting with an imposed system – not something they can amend in the light of local conditions or experience. As a result in many places front line staff are not engaged.

What are the implications and consequences of the system?

Many consequences of the current performance management system have been identified and discussed above. This section concentrates on broader impacts, rather than the specifics of the PAF or the assessment process. A number of questions are posed.

Do the reported performances against PIs tell us about real performance?

There are several reasons why the reported performance against any PI might mislead. The list below of suggestions explaining inaccuracy and non performance related variations between authorities draws heavily from the work of Pearce and King (op. cit.). Misleading characteristics of reported performance include:

- Relative affluence of the area or geographical characteristics. (areas with high numbers of terraced houses for instance are likely to have higher residential placement levels as such houses are less amenable to adaptation).
- Level of national funding.
- Traditions of service provision and the availability of local services.
- The strength of determination within the leadership to improve PI performance.
- The ability of senior managers to tell the local performance story (which rests on their own understanding of the meaning of the reported performance).
- The ability and determination of senior managers to grab the attention of junior managers.
- Competence of managers.
- Level of understanding of definitions (which might rest on the strength of links with DoH, DFES or CSCI or the strength of local networking between information staff in different authorities).
- Thresholds of eligibility chosen.
- The quality of information systems.
- The penetration of understanding of and commitment to the use of information systems and the recording of data.
- Staffing shortages.

This list only goes to confirm that figures reported against the PIs should be used as indicators, and not treated as 'performance'.

Does 'star blight' stifle initiative?

Any organisation with a highly regarded acquired status vulnerable to losing that status can be forgiven for being a little nervous. Three star CSSRs are scared of losing a star, just as two star and one star CSSRs are determined to achieve more. Officers I have spoken to in several three star CSSRs confirm that the nervousness of slipping back is such that the temptation is strong to continue to operate on the basis they achieved their status. Maddock's view that performance measurement relying on outputs does not encourage risk taking or innovation adds weight to this (Maddock, 2002). I have even heard that people in three star organisations say they miss inspections, because inspections keep people on their toes.

Does this pressure merely breed conformity? For the low achievers there is the pressure to conform more to succeed against the process. And is it divisive? Do staff in three star LAs feel as validated as their bosses by the 'success'? Who gets blamed in low achieving LAs by 'failure'? All parts of an authority in special measures are judged to be poor, however good individual services are. Similarly, all parts of three star CSSRs are treated as if they were excellent. This fails to identify in practical terms how much difference in quality of service there is between three star and zero star councils.

Will 'star creep' bring the system into disrepute?

As can be seen in the chart below when the first judgements were made in 2002 barely one third of CSSRs were thought worthy of two or three stars. By 2004, 30 months after that, it was the other way round, with only one third seen as unworthy of two or three star status. This 'progress' continued in 2005: so what's the message here?

There are two interpretations. Firstly the face value interpretation is that there has been a staggering improvement in the quality of social services in England in two years. Or it could be that social services are getting better at collecting and reporting the data and responding to the assessment requirement? Or elements of both could be true. It is undoubtedly the case that the introduction of comprehensive information systems improve data collection and reported performance. That being so in a couple of year's time even the worst CSSR is going to be able to produce decent PIs. Whatever the cause, if the reported improvement in services continues at anything like the rate it has, the system will become pointless with all but an incorrigible handful of CSSRs having three stars. It will as a result fall into disrepute.

The CSCI will not allow all CSSRs to claim the top rating and the ways being employed to avoid this are simple. There are two parts to it. First of all expectations are being ratcheted up. Bandings in PIs are regularly reviewed and Key Thresholds are being raised. For instance the threshold performance below which waiting times for assessments for adults would result in a pegging of the overall judgement to 'serving, some people well' were shifted up 5 per cent for 04/05 and another 5 per cent for 05/06. This merely puts pressure on getting specific business processes right. Of course the CSCI could identify 'thresholds', for many more PIs and raise them annually.

Only Get Better?

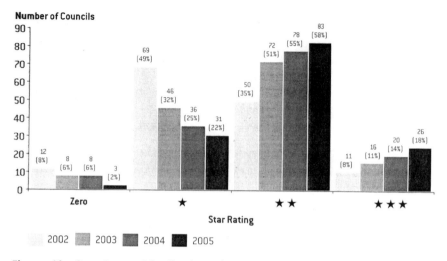

Figure 10   Star Creep. Distribution of star ratings between 2002 and 2005. *Social Services Performance Assessment Framework Indicators* **(CSCI, 2005a)**

Secondly something introduced by the Audit Commission for 05/06 could be borrowed for the social care star ratings. From 05/06 each local authority had their CPA rating refreshed, their performance from then on being rated in stars – zero to four stars. In addition a judgement was published about the 'direction of travel'. This could either be 'progressing strongly', 'progressing well', 'making only limited progress' or 'falling back'. This judgement is not incorporated into the overall score but stands alone. In effect it differentiates between those local authorities achieving the same rating. Being judged an 'Excellent' authority but 'making only limited progress' sounds a lot worse than being 'Excellent', and 'progressing strongly'. If authorities want to see the process as a competition (and they will) they will be able to see who is A – and who is A+. This sort of differentiation could easily be introduced into the social care judgements. The CSCI are considering introducing judgements for each adult service user group; learning disability, physical disability etc, an excellent opportunity for making the overall test harder.

And to the question, where does it all end, the answer is of course that it doesn't. The differentiation can become finer and finer. One impact of this refinement process, if the broad dataset currently collected remains in place, is that the margin for error for social services managers reporting performance becomes slimmer. This inevitably means that CSSRs will pay much more detailed attention to what each PI means, the detail of the definition, implications of changes and so on. CSSRs likely to be affected by changes proposed by the CSCI are bound to question those which might affect their performance, lobby for refinements which suit them and argue against interpretations which do not. This has already happened with the 'Helped to Live at Home' PI series (PAF AO/C29, C30, C31 and C32) for adults. These four PIs require CSSRs to report on the number of vulnerable people who have been assessed under Fair Access criteria (i.e. those who have received a community care assessment) and who receive services which help them remain independent within their own home. However there was for some years debate about which people could be counted. Confusingly in 2002 many CSSRs inferred from comments from the old SSI that CSSRs should include in the PIs people who had received support such as that provided by voluntary agencies funded from the CSSR, but without a community care assessment. But the definition, which clearly stated that only properly assessed people should be counted, was never changed. The result of this was that by 2004 about half the CSSRs were counting it one way and the other half the other. As you could count many more people by including non assessed services the reported performance of the CSSRs which did that was much better. The CSSRs which were reporting accurately were, of course, reporting much less activity than the others and were placed as a result in lower bandings. Not happy about this, several local authorities raised this with the CSCI who in 2004 announced that the definition was to stay the same and that all CSSRs should only count properly assessed people in the return. As a result there was pressure from those previously 'over' reporting that their bandings would be badly affected in the 04/05 reporting round. More debate followed but the bandings were left as they were by the CSCI, as it was pointed out by those who had been reporting accurately (and suffering the consequences for several years), that asking for the scoring to be changed because you had been, in effect, misreporting was a bit rich. There was mild chagrin about this decision and some unease as these PIs are BVPIs as well as PAF PIs (which means they have a higher profile with the CPA process and can be audited externally). Some CSSR's performance against these PIs dropped considerably in 04/05 as a result. As small differences between reported performance become more crucial, and as many officers in CSSRs become as expert as CSCI, DoH and DfES analysts there will be more of this pressure in future.

'Star Creep' is a problem then, which can be overcome, but which will certainly entail a lot of lobbying by CSSRs and forensic examination of definitional changes. In short there may be in future a lot of internal 'gaming' – more effort directed at the system than at improving services.

Targeting or breasting the tape?

There is another implication here, which will become more obvious once the local government efficiency measures begin to bite. The introduction of the

PAF and annual assessment has coincided with the longest sustained increase in social care funding since the early 1970s. Once social services became accustomed to budget increases spending has broadly matched priorities. The priorities which required additional services to be commissioned have been tracked by high profile PIs. Setting targets each year for these PIs was simply a matter of judging how many more service users could be 'collected' and recorded. In that sense 'setting targets' was the wrong phrase. What was required was to identify a winning post each year, with not much concern expressed about how far beyond the winning post the CSSR went. But with financial pressures returning to add to performance pressures setting a specific target and meeting it precisely will be required. Setting targets therefore becomes a more demanding exercise than it has been up to now.

Is continuous improvement achievable?

This brings me to the notion of 'continuous improvement'. The Best Value regime incorporated an explicit expectation that local authorities would demonstrate 'continuous improvement'. Since 1998 neither the AC nor the CSCI for the social care world have issued any statement contradicting this aim. Indeed the AC's document revamping the CPA process *A Harder Test*, published in June 2005 reiterated the demand that continuous improvement be one of every local authority's goals (Audit Commission, 2005c). In strictly human terms continuous improvement is a psychological impossibility. Our everyday experience tells us that when we are learning something new we do not just get better and better. Athletes do not proceed from personal best to personal best. These common sense observations are confirmed by psychological literature. The Yerkes/Dodson studies, a hundred years old now, demonstrated that the relationship between effort and performance in human endeavour is one that produces a tailing off of improvement (Yerkes and Dodson, 1908). Of course organisations are not human beings and can rearrange resources to keep directing effort to achieve a goal. There is the potential here, if the focus remains on continuously improving a small number of PIs, that the focus of effort is entirely skewed, redirecting effort towards the PI (which becomes more demanding as time goes on) rather than service improvement. But there are more subtle concerns as well, because the judgement about whether continuous improvement has been achieved is made on that completely artificial notion – the annual cycle.

The annual round of financial and business planning in both private and public sector is a demanding master, generally understood to result on occasion in short term planning rather than purposeful effort across a number of years to achieve a goal. The government's switch to financial allocation for public services on a three year cycle in 1999 helped to alleviate annual pressures. Moreover the identification in National Service Frameworks of targets for various activities to be reached in three and five years speaks to the need for organisations to gear themselves up for long term change. So there is a potential charge against the current system that annual performance assessments endorse an approach which is short term and reactive rather than encouraging genuine long term planning.

On the same theme although the CSCI's stated aim is to produce 'mature outcome oriented organisations', the opposite may be the result of the tightening annual process, as organisations are less likely to discern what policies and strategies would be good for local people because they have learned just to follow the national lead. This is a strong charge which I think is not entirely the case. But the argument can be made.

Can we record activity well enough? The Information Panopticon

In the early 19th century Jeremy Bentham, social reformer and polymath, took a North American idea and with it designed a new type of prison. Taken up by the authorities, Bentham's Panopticon ('see all') prisons had several long rectangular halls, two or three storeys deep, each storey having parallel rows of cells facing each other across an open landing. Each cell block spread out like a spoke from a central hub, so that one guard at the centre could see the doors of hundreds of prison cells on several levels to left and right, forward and behind. As such any hint of trouble could be spotted immediately and tiny numbers of guards could control hundreds of prisoners. With the PAF and other data collected from local authorities the DoH and DfES have devised an information panopticon, enabling them to look into every corner of the social care landscape. The performance measurement and assessment process allows the government to more easily control local authority services and this panopticon is the main platform upon which the process rests. Lest this comment implies sinister motives to the Labour administration it must be said that all central governments attempt to make local authorities bend to their will.

The difference today is that for the first time the government has been able to achieve a degree of success in what some might call the micromanagement of social care. This has been possible because government departments are now more confident that they know in some detail each CSSR's achievements, what targets it has set for the coming year and what its performance problems are. Although the centre does not have this data in anything like 'real time' (the phrase used by information professionals to mean 'immediately') the delay in the availability of national data is short enough now for it to be useful for planning purposes rather than just for retrospective comment. This is a firm step along the road to comprehensive leadership of both policy and practice. It represents a fundamental development in social care and should not be underestimated.

All this has been made possible by the availability of cheap, simple, widely available IT applications. Neither the PAF nor the annual assessment cycle could happen without them. This availability has both stimulated and been the vehicle for a whole clutch of high level policy developments across local government since 1997, including the e-govt agenda, the NHS Connecting for Health programme and the CPA.

In response to expectations about data collection and reporting, from about 1998 many CSSRs have introduced a whole range of IT applications for operational purposes at breakneck speed. Most of them needed to, because very few were prepared for the information demands laid on them in the late 1990s. Consider for instance the report produced by Social Information Systems for the London Borough of Hillingdon in September 1999. I quote from this not in criticism of Hillingdon. On the contrary looking at their information failings so systematically shows foresight, candour and courage. I have undertaken no systematic survey but would suggest that the information disarray SIS found in Hillingdon was typical of CSSRs at the time. It contains a startling picture of a CSSR in which 'essential basic information [is] not available through any systematic means'. One small section exemplifies, I believe, the picture across the whole country at the time:

> *Under investment in [the service user database] in terms of money, time, commitment etc has had two major effects. Firstly, a classic downward spiral has occurred where lack of engagement with a system has led to poor data quality, justifying lack of engagement and so on. As a result data quality in some areas is obviously poor and unreliable. Secondly, as a response to an inadequate core system, uncontrolled development of alternative local databases, spreadsheets and all manner of manual systems has become widespread. This has had the inevitable consequence that the majority of information being recorded has been inconsistently defined, often multiply recorded and may be impossible to aggregate accurately for the purposes of management reports and statutory returns.*

> *Much . . . time and energy expended in this activity appears to be devoted to reconciliation of information from different systems . . . up to 20% of all management and administrative time.*

LB Hillingdon, 1999.

The report was commissioned partly to prepare the department to respond adequately to the PAF, Quality Protects and RAP, then all brand new. A five year vision was devised for Hillingdon which, unusually, included a comprehensive attempt to re-identify what core business was and ensure a single integrated IT application was available to record data. Although few CSSRs formulated such an all-inclusive vision the necessary interrelationship between operations, information and performance was already becoming clear. At around this time the SSI began to look critically at the quality of recording in CSSRs and laid out guidance under the broad heading of Recording With Care. There was also a steadily increasing number of Subject Access Requests under the Data Protection Act in the late 1990s, then the Information Referral and Tracking project (IRT, later ISA) identified requirements under *Every Child Matters* for a single accessible system to maintain data about all children across the land. Finally in 2001 a timetable was announced by the DoH for the institution in each CSSR of an Electronic Social Care Record (ESCR) by 2006. The case in each council for developing or buying a service user database which served as a complete case record and produced management and performance information was by about 2000 overwhelming. Development of such comprehensive systems is at different stages in different authorities, but the goal, which now includes data sharing with partner agencies, video and audio capacity and direct service user access to records is being approached at speed.

Despite progress the quality of data produced and reported by CSSRs is still a problem. A 2005 audit by the AC examining the quality of the data underlying 'a key group of seven social service PAF indicators' looked at data in seven authorities. The report concluded:

Most social services departments in the audit have significant problems in recording reliable and quality assured data, but there is no evidence of deliberate misreporting. A majority of the key indicators are based on unreliable data; management arrangements for performance information vary. Assessment and inspection conclusions that rely upon these data without supplementary judgement may also be adversely affected.

The report concluded that:

Councils need to give significantly more attention to ensuring data accuracy and completeness to enable them and inspectorates to be confident that performance information . . . can be relied upon. Performance management processes are too variable and reporting is inconsistent. Operational staff frequently lack the training and guidance necessary to make good use of the data.

Audit Commission, 2005.

Those responsible for the Adult Social Care Information Development Programme, launched in 2005 to improve and streamline data collection and data collection methods make even more damning comments:

It is widely recognised amongst key stakeholders both nationally and locally that the current statistical collections on adult social care services do not provide an accurate picture of adult social care activity or the outcomes of that care. Furthermore, the available information does not provide a sound basis for measuring or monitoring performance of social services.

ASCID, 2005.

As the CSCI and AC have been 'measuring and monitoring performance' using this data, this admission is startling. While it is true that approaches to data quality in CSSRs vary immensely, in broad terms the main reason for the difficulties can be laid at the door of government agencies. Before 2005 there had been little concrete help from either the CSCI or AC. The AC have signally failed to put in place robust arrangements for the auditing of BVPIs, some of which are the same as PAF PIs. In theory if the data is wanting the relevant performance indicator can be 'qualified', which means that it is removed from the reckoning in the annual judgements made. This of course can be devastating to an authority. In my experience the level of knowledge amongst local auditors is variable and the system for getting results of their activities is flawed – on one occasion at least I am aware of the results of the audit activity into PIs being made available after the annual social service judgement had been published. This is regrettable when so much rides on aspects of the judgements made on the basis of this data. The Audit Commission, working with the CSCI, are attempting to offer guidance with a self assessment tool promoting data quality published in April 2005. This might have some impact on data quality and indicates a willingness to work with Local Authorities on what is a key issue in performance measurement (Audit Commission, 2005).

So we a have a nest of paradoxes. The government has set up an information panopticon. Government agencies act as if the information is robust, judging and criticising local authorities on the back of it. At the same time there is a general understanding that there are serious problems with the quality of the data reported. But government agencies have been slow to expend the effort to improve it.

How compatible is IT with social care?

The basis of successful data collection and reporting are the IT systems used to gather the data, so we need to consider how mass IT applications have been introduced in social care. I imagine anyone working in social care has, like me, heard the sort of comments listed below:

- 'I didn't come into this job to be a typist . . .'
- 'I've not had proper training to do this . . .'
- 'Who's put this together? It bears no relation to the work I do at all . . .'
- 'It takes me hours filling these things in. I've counted 327 clicks just to get the referral form done'.

But although there are many complaints along these lines it must not be thought that the response of social care staff to such applications is simply Luddite. It's more sophisticated than that, and will also include demands such as:

- 'Why can't I do so and so on this system? Why can't we have up to date technology?
- 'Why does the screen look so geeky? Why can't we have something flasher?'
- 'Why can't we be involved in devising the application?'

There are six major reasons for problems with the implementation of IT applications and its use. First of all what is required for social care, is a complex hybrid application. The average social care service user data base has been specified to:

- Hold demographic data about large numbers of individuals.
- Hold scores of fields of additional data about these people, each requiring different sorts of information.
- Establish multiple navigation routes through a single record.
- Ensure that the individual fields are not only linked internally, but can be easily navigated.
- Be secure, not just keeping data from prying eyes from outside the organisation but having access filtered to different people internally.
- Ensure updating from multiple sources can be achieved.
- Devise access methods from identified and trusted outsiders from partner organisations, and devise ways for these outsiders to update certain sections of the record.
- Ensure that data can be collated in many different configurations, ensuring that 50 or 60 different data sets can be interrogated and reports produced for any conceivable chronological period.
- Raise warnings about activity required by certain deadlines, both within the individual record and by e-mail to a list of others.
- Carry warnings about the status of individuals recorded on the system.

A complicating factor is that although the specification broadly required by each council is similar there is no overarching specification to secure compatible systems across the country. Each council sets its own specification and buys its own. Unlike the centralised approach being tested out by the NHS with the Connecting for Health project these arrangements seem a little ragged.

The second problem has been the speed of introduction of all embracing systems. From an occupation which in 1998 did not have much to do with computers, many social care staff are now expected to manage all their day to day recording on a single IT application. In this regard social care staff are miles ahead of the overwhelming majority of their colleagues in health organisations. But there have been casualties and confrontations. Poor recording, bad data quality, work stress and resignations have resulted.

Much has been made of the aging nature of social service workforces, as well as the proposal that social work is somehow inimical to the use of computers to explain these difficulties. But most difficulties with IT systems have been caused by the third problem – lack of basic preparation. The design, testing and implementation of aspects of social care databases need the involvement of front line staff, the people who are to use the systems. But not enough front line staff have been released to help write specifications and test systems out. Initially it seems many systems transferred operational procedures directly into the navigation pathway of the IT application. That would be alright if the people doing the job followed procedures as they are written down. But they don't. They ignore bits, slide round other sections, and do things slightly differently from what it says in the book. This doesn't matter in a world of manual recording – human beings are naturally imaginative and flexible. But if these written procedures are translated into an electronic recording system, as they often have been, a bureaucratic monster is created. IT systems are unforgiving and will not let users slide round bits they don't need to complete. Thus, many service user databases designed partly to speed things up have inevitably slowed them down to a frustrating procession of button clicking and data entry about issues staff have little understanding of and no commitment to. The performance measurement aspects of this agenda have been among the most frustrating for front line staff. Many service user databases are the primary vehicle now for the data which is collated to form the PAF PIs. As many PAF PIs look at timeliness, the date which data is entered is absolutely crucial. Similarly recording the ethnic status of service users has been since 2005/06 a Key Threshold, so every CSSR has to be extremely careful about this. Social workers rail against having to, as some put it, ask people what their ethnic background is when they feel they should be concentrating on the child protection investigation, or the carer whose mother has just suffered a life threatening stroke. Some of course will not raise this question – it gets lost in the crisis and in many cases post hoc 'blitzes' of ethnic status fields are undertaken by admin staff who are encouraged to 'guess' what the ethnic status was.

The performance measurement requirements built into service user databases and the traditional secondary status of recording in social care has therefore contributed to the difficulties experienced by front line staff. As technology develops these inappropriate aspects of IT applications may be massaged away, but for the moment even the most sophisticated systems are very demanding, One group of managers I know of who are committed to the system they use, nevertheless spend so much time managing their teams' caseloads in front of a screen they refer to themselves as 'click-bunnies'.

Underlying these practical concerns is a more subtle disquiet. This fourth problem is the emotional impact of wholesale computerisation. Social care work has traditionally relied upon the worker's brain and heart. Practice models, procedures and hypotheses about human behaviour might help, but the source of decent social work is still seen as the personality and character of the worker. Unlike many community health staff social workers' use of tools and scales is relatively limited. The unfiltered relationship between worker and the people needing help is the vehicle for that work. I remember, when I started as a probation officer, one of my colleagues declined to send typewritten letters to her clients because she thought the formality of the typed letter got in the way. She hand wrote them instead. That may have taken the romance of the individual relationship a little far (and it was a long time ago) but was a perfectly understandable position to take for all that. Today the PC, or increasingly the laptop, is the primary working tool of the social worker. Does that get in the way?

Some would say it does in a severely practical sense. 'I'm not going to open up my lap top in Mrs Smith's house', Cath says, 'how would that look?' Cath argues that it might be alright for young fellows selling mortgages to open up their laptops in front of people in their own homes but it would be inappropriate for her to do the same considering the sensitivity of some of the discussions she has to have with people. This goes back to the 'commodification' of social care discussed earlier. No other occupational group would think twice about this. Is there some mystique in social work that makes this an issue?

Perhaps something to do with IT itself conflicts with social workers' views – humanity in the raw meeting hard edged technology. This confrontation, the fifth problem, is encapsulated in the language of the two occupations. In social care we deal with human beings in distress or who have overwhelming incapacities. Our language is therefore careful, sometimes ambiguous and not often final. We talk of the potential for change, of care plans evolving and struggle with moving family relationships on. Our goals tend to be either tiny behavioural hints or broader signifiers of a capacity to take responsibility or grasp just a little more independence. It is different in IT. The first time I heard a rep from an IT company talk of his company's 'Solution', I puzzled at what he meant. Did he mean some sort of glue? It slowly became clear that what he was referring to as the 'Solution' was the piece of software developed for the particular purpose we had specified – the product he was trying to sell us. When I understood him I was shocked, not just that his use of the word was premature but that he should be so arrogant as to use this word in such an ambitious sense. But of course he was not being arrogant – he was merely using an industry standard word. I hear it all the time, but it grates on me just as the North American use of the word 'closure' (to mean the final resolution of a great trauma) does. In social care use of words in this pushy way implies an emotional shallowness. In IT it's just business. But confusion over language can get us all off on the wrong foot, gnawing away at any initial goodwill. This is not just semantics. As Ezra Pound said, 'if language goes rotten, everything goes rotten' (Sutch, 2005). More attention needs to be given to the way professionals talk to each other.

But this sort of dissonance is not just noticeable between the worlds of social care and IT but also, and this is the sixth problem, within social care about IT. Despite the difficulties I have highlighted above there is an emerging IT literacy in social care organisations. But this developing maturity causes problems of its own. Front line staff understand the workings of the electronic database they are using and senior managers tend not to. These are so new no senior manager will ever have had to use one. So senior managers in social care organisations, for the first time, have no real idea what front line work is really like; what dominates the working day, what infuriates, what rewards. Can they manage their staff and the business without detailed knowledge of how day to day work is carried out? The answer has to be yes, of course. Managers are not simply super practitioners. However I wonder if some of today's managers still think they understand the pressures on the front line and act accordingly, and confusingly – when they have only a limited idea.

Challenges and fragilities

The consideration of the role of IT in social care, as part of the performance measurement and assessment regime, has taken up considerable space. This is more than justified because the whole performance measurement process is predicated on good IT. In spite of all the problems outlined above social care has taken to the demands on it more positively than can have been hoped. Yet the PAF is still relatively new. Everybody, even the CSCI, DfES and DoH, are still getting accustomed to it. It's not surprising therefore that there are many frustrations. Those not considered above include:

- There are a developing set of disciplines related to performance measure-ment, but as the process is only eight years old in social care there is no professional place for it. As it has developed, higher profile posts have been created that incorporate responsibility for performance 'management', but these tend to be lumped together with finance or HR or planning. I would not suggest the development of a separate professional specialism, when the process probably should be led by operational managers and when performance is said to be everyone's responsibility. But there is a structural conundrum – things that are everyone's responsibility are often no one's.

- The Chancellor announced in his budget statement in 2005 that the 11 public service inspectorates will be reduced to four by 2008, with the CSCI merging with the Health Care Commission and a completely new children's inspectorate being created. This creates huge questions; will social care concerns be swamped by the juggernaut of health on the one hand and the steamroller of education on the other?
- The Annual Performance Assessment for all children's services run by local authorities (not just social care services) and the ambitious Joint Area Reviews are the first attempt to make serious judgements across organisational boundaries. Something similar will no doubt follow for adult services with the proposed amalgamation of the CSCI and Health Care Commission. This will involve complexities yet to be unravelled, but needs to be attempted. The previous silo approach to performance assessment services which rely on partnership working has been a serious weakness.
- The focus on clear service outcomes for both children's services and adult's will sharpen further over the coming years. The CSCI will therefore have to measure how good CSSRs are at really making things better for people as a result of CSSR support. This is a very sophisticated requirement discussed in the next chapter.
- All inspectorates are making great play of the lighter touch they will be using, the reduction in reporting requirements, fewer PIs and an increased reliance on self assessment by CSSRs. While welcome this raises questions about the maintenance of quality if the inspection and assessment function shrinks. The CSCI is still new and is dominated by managers whose background is in regulation, i.e. people who managed homes inspectors. Many of the old technocrats from the SSI who put the performance assessment system together have left as pay rates have fallen and staff have been shed. Business Relationship Managers newly appointed to the CSCI seem to be from relatively junior social care positions. Does the CSCI (or any successor body), with fewer staff with less experience on lower salaries, have the capacity to make an increasingly sophisticated performance measurement and assessment process work?

Before the 2005 general election the Conservative party made promises about doing away with 'targets' in public services, particularly health. The Conservatives also criticised the bloated waste, as they saw it, of the 'inspection' industry which they suggested in 2005 was costing an estimated £1 billion a year. (The government quickly countered by claiming the cost was closer to £90m). Add to this the professional criticisms of performance measurement, the public distrust debated above and the various infelicities of the current system and it might be thought that the assessment and performance process in health and social care is very fragile. But the political expectation that services meet particular standards and service commissioners are tested against those standards is by no means spent. Also, and this is the crucial factor, as we saw above in the government's terms this process works. Local Authorities respond to the demands of the system and that's a great prize. No government, of whatever colour, is likely to discard something that offers them the opportunity to lead and control.

Overall thesis

The several themes discussed above can be summarised in eight points:

1. Social care policy is now entirely centrally directed – this has only been the case since 1998. Local discretion is less than it has ever been.
2. This has been made possible by the general availability of cheap, simple IT applications.
3. The process of central direction and the performance assessment process has delivered some benefits to service users and has sharpened the focus of CSSRs.
4. This is a political tool. The information panopticon has allowed politicians to lead decisively.
5. The pressures of performance measurement and assessment on CSSRs are louder than the demands of service users.
6. However carefully integrated into the life of the organisation the performance measurement and performance assessment regime skews the direction of effort in CSSRs.
7. The quality of much of the data reported to central government is questionable. Even though government offices share these concerns, ministers and the CSCI act as if they have reliable data.
8. Although performance measurement processes offer benefits to organisational aims the stark imposition of processes on CSSRs from the centre is its major weakness. Many staff feel alienated from the aims and practices imposed on them.

Exercise

Ask your team and your colleagues two, two part questions:

- Identify the ways that the performance measurement system has improved services to users or improved your job.
- Identify the ways that the performance measurement system has made your job more difficult or threatened the service to users.

List the positives and negatives separately for the service and for your job. Compare and debate the two sets of lists.

Chapter 5

How Can it be Improved?

I fear the big words . . . that make us so unhappy.

James Joyce, *Ulysses*

Despite the criticisms above there is no suggestion here that performance measurement processes developed over the last decade should be abandoned. There are, no doubt, arguments to be made for replacing this bureaucratic process completely. But this is a practically oriented book, which can offer help to those struggling with contemporary reality, so the debate below is set within the current framework. The expectations of government in measuring performance may have been off beam occasionally but not as off beam as the previous lack of openness, lack of focus, lack of information and low level of public accountability. The processes used have not been perfect, but as a CSCI manager said to me 'it is an imperfect world'. Those imperfections can be improved to make something real for the human beings at the centre of the system. But this requires a shift in thinking and greater ambition.

A major shift required is for policy makers to recognise the conundrum at the heart of the government's emerging policy for social care. The ambition that councils should develop tailored responses to each individual is articulated in grand, centrally driven policies. Yet the link between that ambition and the desperation of the abused child or despair in the face of a degenerative illness is sometimes hard to discern. The modernisation agenda, expressed partly in the performance assessment and performance measurement processes can only make sense to people – staff as well as recipients of services – if it is interpreted on a human scale. The big words are just too big to make sense to most of us. And policy directives often leave the impression on the front line that these things are not to do with them. Also the link between policy and end result, the Golden Thread of Audit Commission legend, is always explained and interpreted as a thread falling from the top of the organisation to the front line. And this thread may not be seen as the lifeline it was to Theseus in the Minotaur's Labyrinth but a chain dragging staff along with it. This does not support workers to help ordinary people in distress – even though the front line worker is the most crucial aspect of any performance improvement initiative. Performance improvement processes must be more inclusive than the command and control approach imposed on

CSSRs so far. Something more responsive has to be created, not just ambitions that make sense to people, but a way of ensuring that all those involved are convinced about pulling in the same direction. So let's forget the Golden Thread and think more of establishing a 'co-operative community', where co-ordinated activity can be seen to lead to real improvements in how people live their lives. The latter part of the chapter contains thoughts about how such 'communities' might be established.

But first staff need to understand and work with the bureaucracy within which those ideas are currently played out. So this chapter is divided into three sections; the first includes advice for front line staff about how to live with what is, the second suggests ways that ideas from practice can be used in concert with performance measurement disciplines and the third has ideas for managers and the CSCI about turning a measurement and assessment process into something more suited to frail humanity than unyielding corporations.

Learning to swim with the tide

The exercises at the end of Chapter 1 were aimed at helping individuals identify performance improvement processes in their own lives. The proposition was that in order to improve any activity, that activity has to mean something to people and they have to have the will and power to change it. The implications of this are simple for performance measurement in social care. The attention of front line staff has to be grabbed and some power devolved to them. But to do that considerable preparations have to be made across the organisation.

The most important starting point is engaging in a discussion about the process; the detail as well as the big ideas. So regular briefings have to take place about plans, objectives, measures, targets and so on. This should be part of the ordinary life of the organisation. More specifically the relationship between high level plans, team level processes and the work of the teams should be spelled out. Thus for the objective of improving the choice and independence of frail older people in their accommodation the following strata of objectives and processes might help staff link what they do with what senior managers talk about. The example used here is the aim of improving the independence of frail older people.

The high level outcome required can be identified as ensuring the long term support for independent living for frail older people. Bearing in mind the association of residential care with raised levels of depression and reduced capacity for independent living one key objective should be that less reliance should be placed on residential care for older people.

Service level outcomes might therefore include the aim of fewer people being placed in residential care, an increase in support and care in the home, additional arrangements made for 'extra care' arrangements in housing and imaginative use of Supporting People funding. But service level outcomes must not just transfer institutional style care into people's own homes.

Organisational processes might include additional payments for domiciliary care agencies which support very frail people, integrated hospital discharge teams, block contracting for support in crisis, and the establishment of community support networks. This approach should be explained to and discussed with providers and to local people. Satisfaction surveys or measures of independence levels amongst service users might also be deployed.

Team level processes to implement the policy might include resources to put together and manage complex integrated packages of care, regular meetings with NHS staff to ensure tight relationships exist, regular panels to monitor residential placements and quality audits to check on levels of independence.

Service user outcomes should include evidence of maintained or increased levels of independent living and contentment with support and care arrangements.

There are clear messages here for managers about the need to link team processes to service aims to overall objectives. However for staff the message is if what you are asked to do does not makes sense to you then you have to demand some explanation. Moreover if what you are being asked to do is not accompanied with adequate training and support that support should be demanded. 'Demand' is a fiery word to suggest to front line staff – but it is justified if anyone is asked to do anything they either do not understand or goes against their conscience or conflicts with their practice experience.

Once such explanations have been offered and supports are in place, the way the performance measurement processes are played out can be monitored by front line staff by checking local performance procedures against six performance principles. These are:

1. Activity to meet targets should not affect service users.
2. Activity to meet targets should not be burdensome to staff. No double data entry should be required for case recording on the one hand and performance measurement on the other.
3. Relevant indicators must be understood in detail at team level, as should targets.
4. Information about team progress against PIs should be made regularly available to team members.
5. There must be a way of including front line staff in the debate about improvements, target setting and so on.
6. Front line staff must be able to see a congruent relationship between reported performance, good practice and good outcomes for people.

The first principle is a check against perversity in performance. We saw in chapter one the suggestion that Abel's plan to move a young man from a failing placement was delayed because of the pressure of PI CF/A1 *The stability of placements of children looked after*. If the proposed move was delayed for even a half an hour because of the PI, that is not acceptable. PIs should 'indicate' activity not dominate it. And while it is acceptable to review and amend processes in the light of the requirements of the PI it is not acceptable that the needs of the PI override the needs of individual service users.

The second principle relates primarily to the way activity is recorded. While it is reasonable for service user databases to include the recording of data for a PI, it is not acceptable for any separate record to be required for performance purposes. Record once, but use the data a million times. Never record twice.

The third is self evident and was discussed above. The targets required however should also be interpreted for each team. Within a CSSR there may be variations in demography, affluence or patterns of referrals for a range of reasons; housing stock, availability of particular types of service and so on. So targets set for the whole CSSR have to be internally interpreted. Some teams may be seriously challenged by some targets that are eminently reasonable in other teams. Sub targets are crucial therefore to keep teams appropriately engaged.

The corollary of this, the fourth principle, is that each team should be informed regularly of how it is doing against the target. This is also important so staff can take control of their own work and their own learning (Raine and Wilson, 1997). This is a major failing in many CSSRs.

The fifth is common sense. Front line staff know what is going on, know service users, know the pressures on them. Not to include them in discussions of targets and processes is unacceptable.

The sixth principle, encapsulates them all. It is this last on which the establishment of a co-operative community is predicated. Good practice should lead to good outcomes, and should lead to good reported performance. If all three aspects of this triad of meaning are congruent then the process is working. But if good reported performance is based on poor outcomes or if practice has to be skewed to produce good reported performance then questions have to be asked.

Using these principles the requirements of front line staff are straightforward. Staff need to:

- Demand clarity about exactly what is expected of them.
- Ensure they know the organisational priorities and how they relate to their own work. This is a management responsibility as much as the team's.
- Understand how to record, when to record, what to record.

- Know precisely which PIs relate to their team.
- Know how the whole process hangs together.
- Receive regular feedback about PI performance.
- Know their local story. If they are falling down on a PI why is that? Is that up to the team, or local demography, sickness levels, staffing shortages, referral patterns, etc.
- Take all opportunities to contribute to the debate about how to do things better, improve processes, or change the PIs.
- Raise regularly any evidence of dissonances between good practice, good outcomes and good reported performance.

But it is as important to look at performance outside the formal PAF process as well. The exercise at the end of Chapter 2 was designed to provide an opportunity for people to compare their own view of the critical outcomes of the team with those measures and targets included in the PAF PIs. Every team should have a clear idea of what its aims are, in addition to the criteria used in the external performance judgements. Identify your own measures, so you know how you are doing against your own criteria and those of the service users you work with. Such measures do not have to be sophisticated or even statistical, but must be explicit. Perhaps, using your own criteria, there are ways you can demonstrate to managers how well you are doing, which are either additional to or which are at a tangent to the PAF system. But walk before you can run. And walking means that as a team you must be collecting the data required for the PAF PIs in a timely and responsible manner. No one will take you seriously if you don't. There is no choice here. Even if the wrong activities are counted and the analysis of these activities is flawed, to function properly any organisation needs to account for, and therefore count, its activities.

The exercises at the end of chapter three concentrated on the language of performance measurement, identifying what it means and helping people understand their own local performance situation. Language and locality are key factors in helping people manage in the world of PIs. Think back to Cath's situation in Chapter 1. She carried out work with the most demanding older people. Her boss however made no allowance for that and operated a quota system for the number of residential admissions allowed. Local knowledge in this case may have indicated that Cath was likely to have to consider admission more often than her colleagues. Could not allowance be made for that? The PAF is a monolithic imposition, but can and should be interpreted flexibly within CSSRs.

Beth's problem in Chapter 1 with the completion of initial assessments and Dev's with health checks for teenage boys both demand a fresh look at the way those aspects of the work are managed within their authority. Why is the advice given to Beth to 'pretend' the timing taken to complete assessments is shorter than it is? Managers should review processes and make sure assessments can be completed on time. And why is Dev managing health checks personally? Why are there not arrangements in place for these checks to be managed by a central unit automatically? Ephraim, the Review Officer's problem is the simplest. He should know the deadlines for all his cases and act upon them.

Diving in: making performance measurement work for you

If the primary principle of viable performance measurement is to establish congruence between good outcomes, good practice and good reported performance, one of the requirements to achieve this is to establish a relationship between the big world of national priorities and performance targets and the small worlds of individuals and families needing help. This requires that we reconcile the measurement of the quantity of any activity with any judgement about its impact on service users – the quality of the service.

Osbourne and Gaebler's aphorism 'what gets measured gets done' is often quoted by managers as a justification for concentrating effort on performance measurement no matter what its impact on people is. Confronted with this sort of attitude many front line staff claim that 'accountants have taken over social work'. And damning what many see as a pathetic numbers game is easy sport. Peter Beresford, the social work academic, in a sideswipe at performance measurement, commented 'My local council has delivered poor services . . . because it has adopted a tick box approach to government targets' (Beresford, 2005). Observations such as this are commonplace and tend to support the naïve proposal that quantitative approaches have no place in any judgement about the outcome of social work and social care practice. But the supposed dichotomy between quality and quantity is not that simple, for quality and quantity are different sides of the same coin. The problem in social care is that traditionally quantity is measured across the organisation while quality of life and satisfaction, seen on the front line everyday, is thought to be almost impossible to measure successfully. In social care quantity and quality live in different realities and not nearly enough has been done to help these two Janus like concepts co-exist.

The CSCI is determined to inject some quality checking into the perform- ance measurement process by identifying PIs which measure 'outcomes' for service users. This is sometimes discussed as if it is something new in social care. But there are dozens of practices which seek precise outcomes and whose outcomes are carefully measured. I will mention a few of these below and will then discuss how such practices might be used to complement and supplement numerical performance indicators.

Warm surveys

Increasingly surveys are required by the CSCI as part of the PAF process, surveys being seen as giving relatively pure measures of outcome. These formal surveys require large samples of service user populations to be approached. Large authorities find themselves sending survey letters to nearly 1000 people. Some of the groups to be surveyed are traditionally difficult to engage and consequently return rates are either poor and/or entail a number of reminders. This effort, and it is considerable effort, cannot result in anything other than simple answers to a dozen or so questions.

These surveys are generally served cold, in the guise of a formal letter. Although the survey can be undertaken on the telephone or by face to face interviews, in practice the cost of doing so compared to using the post is prohibitive. But letters from organisations with power over you, however benignly intended, are not universally welcomed, may elicit 'guarded' responses or may just put people off. It is my experience too that the survey results are seen as just that; results, and results only. They are rarely used as management information that could be the basis of further investigation, but the end of the process, mildly interesting possibly and OK to report for the PI, but nothing more. The results when reported may form the basis for comparison with other authorities, but only as a rudimentary benchmark. The CSCI does allow other questions to be asked as part of the PAF survey, but within a tightly controlled pattern. The guidance makes it clear that the overwhelming purpose is to produce nationally consistent data. So a potentially useful way of engaging people is controlled so tightly that its local use is limited.

Despite the crudity of this approach there is potential here. First of all the PAF expectations mean that English CSSRs are developing fairly uniform expertise in managing surveys. Secondly there is some potential for CSSRs to defray the costs of running individual surveys by forming consortia to run them. Ten authorities running a survey might produce a more professional outcome at less cost and would provide local benchmarking. There are ethical problems to be overcome here, in relation to the confidentiality of the information returned, but nothing insurmountable. But there is no encouragement for this. These big consultation events could also be developed to encourage CSSRs to learn as much from people as they can, to deepen their understanding of people's needs by building other service user consultation activity round them.

But any attempt to get at the real experience of service users has to be done face to face – using that most precious and expensive resource, the human being. There are a huge number of examples of this sort of process used in social care and health. One such is the Speakeasy idea (see Trafford Metropolitan Borough website). This uses groups of trained older people to interview other older people about their needs, circumstances and responses to initiatives. The potential meeting of minds that this approach implies can be developed by ensuring that vernacular language is used in all service user consultation rather than the strained cadences of survey speak. There are also endless examples of satisfaction being gauged in anecdotal or informal ways at the countless meetings, consultation events and visits that members, staff and managers undertake to see how services work. It is difficult to log these encounters in a systematic way, but it is often the comments offered in unguarded moments which have the most resonance.

It would be foolish to suggest that authorities could afford to undertake large number face to face surveys using trained, sensitive, CRB checked people to lead them. It might be managed once possibly, but to mean something such 'warm' surveys would have to be carried out with the same sample on a number of occasions. Nevertheless there is potential to incorporate this sort of approach into the performance measurement approaches currently used. And simply by requiring CSSRs to log all opinions and comments from service users would establish numbers large enough to be able to draw some conclusions from. Alternatively a small number of face to face surveys could be incorporated into the surveys administered by post. This approach would not add much to the centre's knowledge of performance but would be an opportunity to deepen the CSSRs local intelligence. It would also validate or challenge the findings of the larger traditional survey.

Linking performance reporting processes with practice outcomes

Activities such as setting out plans to improve coping mechanisms and checking that change is taking place are at the core of a lot of social work practice. If real links can be made between formal performance reporting and the work done with human beings then the triad of meaning discussed above could be established. At the very least front line staff would more easily be engaged. It's time for CSSRs to consider developing their own measures of success based on successful work done. There are many examples of practice which could be incorporated into a locally evolved outcome oriented performance measurement process.

Care planning

The care planning process by definition identifies desired outcomes and puts plans in place to achieve those outcomes. Reviews and review conferences are ubiquitous practice across all service user groups. All of this activity is recorded and is available for collation. The capture of the aims and outcomes of care plans would be a relatively easy thing to establish and would be a far better measures of success than the cool quantities collected as part of the PAF. The issue here of course is that reviews are often either process dominated events or cursory. The completion of the review to a timetable is often the most pressing feature of it – not the updating of the care plan or the identification of any achievements.

Outcomes and assessment

The debate about how outcomes for service users are defined and how outcome oriented practice can be introduced in care planning owes a lot to Hazel Qureshi and her colleagues at York University. In a series of small scale collaborative exercises new structures for assessments have been developed which lead to care plans with precisely identified outcomes for service users. Tools include prompt lists which remind assessment staff of commonly identified outcomes. Qureshi reports that staff find the frameworks helpful and practical to use and that clear identification of outcomes improved with practice. Such procedures are now becoming commonplace with older people and people with learning disabilities. Qureshi and her colleagues found that predictors of success in developing outcome oriented frameworks were extensive consultation with service users, carers and staff, belief on the part of the staff that the methods were designed to improve practice, a participatory approach to assessment and strong leadership from local managers. The main barriers to the introduction of outcome focussed models were costs of staff training and briefing, the pace of the initiative, and the extent and urgency of other changes. There are outcome models available for work with children and families too, although principally from the US, where individual services have considerable freedom to set their own standards and identify their own performance measures (Wells et al. 2001).

Several local authorities are experimenting with outcome based contracting. Typically the process used for adult service users starts with a community care assessment. Like the 'In Control' idea in learning disability services, an amount of money is allocated as a result of the assessment which can buy what care is needed. The service user, or his or her advocate, then negotiates directly with potential providers about what they do, as their desired outcomes develop or change over the weeks. A running outcome satisfaction log can be maintained by both the agency and the service user. An approach developed in Fareham and Gosport identifies performance thresholds for providers and measures the progress of providers in achieving those thresholds (Ramsay, 2001). This requires much more precise monitoring than is often the norm in social care organisations.

Soft outcomes

Judging the progress made by someone against a Person Centred Plan (PCP) – required in the learning disability world under the Valuing People banner – is more difficult. The PCP is a set of linked notions rather than a formal plan with a template to complete. Such plans are seen as developing organically with the needs of the service user and the recording of such plans is a matter of personal choice. So no one working with people with learning disability would say, 'I've got 25 PCPs done and here are the forms to prove it'. However one of the questions requiring an answer in the 2005 Delivery and Improvement Statement (DIS) was *how many people with a learning disability have a person centred plan?* If the PCP is to be a truly personal plan this is impossible to answer without manipulating and demeaning the very idea of the PCP. Each PCP is a different fruit. This precisely encapsulates the problem of humanising performance measurement. And this is where soft outcomes come in.

The idea of soft outcomes is from adult education and has been interpreted in the world of learning disability. It is of potential use with anyone who has a learning need or a lack of confidence. The idea is to identify by painstaking discussion the levels of confidence and ability of people in minute areas of their lives. So if someone habitually looks away when meeting a person for the first time that is recorded. A matrix of behaviours is recorded and over months of observation, variations in response to all these minute behaviours are recorded. At the same time work is undertaken to help with the person's confidence in agreed areas. And when the occasion comes when the person does not avoid eye contact when meeting someone new that too is recorded. So a detailed record is built up of the soft outcomes of the work done. These, if the work is successful, are the building blocks for hard outcomes like being able to catch a bus.

These ideas are being investigated in depth within the world of adult learning. The Learning and Skills Council (LSC) and National Institute of Adult Continuing Education (NIACE) are jointly leading an initiative called Recognising and Recording Progress and Achievements (RARPA). Designed for adult learners on non assessed courses, RARPA (See RARPA page on NIACE website http://www.niace.org.uk/projects/RARPA/Default.htm) includes a simple model for identifying learning needs at the beginning of a course of study or training, identifying learning goals, checking them throughout the learning activity and at the end. The model used is demanding of teachers because it requires specific attention to each learner. It is a more formal relation of the soft outcomes approach and is something to keep an eye on for its potential use in social care.

Soft outcomes are about helping to manage work to change behaviours at a very human level. The approach is also a quality assurance tool. The changes are only quantifiable through communication with individuals who know the person well. If a hard outcome for an individual is living independently the soft outcomes associated with this might be a wide range of accomplishments such as increased sense of self worth, ability to make more decisions regarding day to day life, more meaningful relationships with neighbours, a healthier lifestyle, confidence to try other things, reduction in behaviours classed as challenging and generally feeling better about life. Person centered planning ideas are completely compatible with a soft outcomes approach. It is the success of the soft outcomes in essence that keeps the statistics of the hard outcomes increasing, for that is how we know that we are moving in the right direction with an individual.

It is difficult to see how this minute and intimate approach could be reconciled with formal performance indicators. To incorporate any sort of recorded soft outcome in any sort of authority wide PI would require the process to be simplified into something it was never intended to be. And yet . . . could there not be a way of collating information about those people achieving soft outcomes within a team area? At least it would identify a direction of travel for those people not achieving the massive stride of, for instance, moving into independent accommodation.

Quality of life

The notion of 'recovery' is being actively discussed in Mental Health. Linked to the idea of quality of life scales the discussion about recovery centres on a set of characteristics which represent improvement after an episode of illness. Simple though this seems the long term nature of much severe and enduring mental illness has pushed such notions into the background in much practice. Quality of life scales, used a great deal in mental health services, also identify sets of characteristics which if used longitudinally can give a clear indication of someone's improving or deteriorating quality of life. But again to 'administer' the procedure properly requires a lot of time from trained and sensitive workers.

Evaluation

Evaluation programmes and quality audits are part of the life of CSSRs. Evaluation disciplines are different from performance measurement but there are also similarities. Blalock points out that performance measurement and evaluation research have developed along parallel but separate paths. She suggests that they can be used in an integrated fashion, enhancing the evidence base of performance indicators and offering higher profile results for evaluations (Blalock, 1999).

Conclusion

Outcome oriented practices and warm surveys require profound attention to the individual and his or her circumstances. Such practices all adopt the premise that change of the individual is possible, desirable and can be achieved as an ordinary part of the work of front line staff. And improved outcomes if recorded can add up to a comprehensive record of improvement across a whole service. But if performance indicators in the PAF mould were overlaid on these practices another hard edged statistical exercise would be created. This, in my view, would inevitably lead to the same pressures and games discussed earlier. And, it might be argued, staff cannot accommodate such a demanding practice focus anymore because they are spending so much time recording data for the PAF PIs which so dominate their lives . . .

Is there a middle way with performance – between tiny human achievements and big number performance assessment processes? While at a tangent to the big ideas in the current performance measurement processes these soft ideas are not antipathetic to them. Perhaps there is a way of developing these ideas to complement one another. It occurs to me that a lot of CSSRs have not incorporated the PAF process into the work of their departments as fully as they could have. Discussions about performance measurement tend to sit apart from the primary work of CSSRs. But there are links between policy development, evaluation audits, developments in contracting, practice improvements and performance measurement – and it doesn't take much imagination to see them.

Diverting the river

I have heard CSCI managers talk of their 'hot pursuit' of 'outcome' PIs. This is not just talk, as in 2006 the CSCI is moving to replace the increasingly discredited PAF PI set with a set of 'outcome' oriented PIs. It is also planning to introduce for 2007/08 a performance assessment framework which takes account of the emerging agenda, emphasising such things as prevention and the use of 'telecare'. Principally however the intention is to move entirely to a set of outcomes as the basis of the judgements made about each CSSR.

But what are these 'outcome' PIs that are being sought so assiduously? As with everything else in social care there is no simple answer. It is understandable that sometimes the idea of a desirable service outcome is confused with service user satisfaction or preference. Simple **satisfaction** with the service is probably the least helpful and most misleading type of outcome to measure. Service users have a limited understanding of what services are available and what they might benefit from – so they have no way of comparing 'satisfaction' of one service with another. Some services users, especially older people, might want to please those asking whether they were satisfied. Others, because they are human beings, might be deliberately belligerent if asked about their service. Some people, and not just disturbed adolescents and people with mental health problems, might deliberately choose to prefer harmful 'outcomes' for themselves or ineffective services. People need guidance and the staff of the CSSR have to continue to offer this guidance along with their professional support.

There is also the social engineering aspect of the PAF and performance assessment process. It has, for instance, been the PAF and the star rating system which has been at the root of the drastic reduction in admissions of older people to residential care over the first five years of the twenty first century. The government introduced the process, partially at least, to 'engineer' social care in a particular direction. That's what policy is. Measurement of outcomes based principally on service user preference and satisfaction would relinquish that policy drive. Would any government willingly give that up? I don't think so.

This does not invalidate asking people what they think, seeking preferences and checking satisfaction. But if the aim is to measure real improvements in services as experienced by service users the impact of measuring reported satisfaction is limited and has to be complemented by other outcome measures. There are other types of outcome which PIs could be devised to measure. These include:

1. The **effectiveness of particular services** in achieving stated outcomes in the original care plan. These of course can either be about maintaining levels of functioning or seeking improvements. This would put a premium as never before on care planning and review processes.
2. A relevant aspect of the **quality of life** of the service user or family such as 'well being' or 'independence' or 'being in control' achieved by individuals as a result of the services offered – as indicated by some sort of regularly administered tool or scale.
3. The **comparative 'social inclusion' achievements** of complete service user populations compared with the general population. For this and the previous outcome there is a question of attributability. How would we know whether a particular service was at the root of any achievement or improvement in the quality of the service user's life?

There many variants on these themes. For a comprehensive debate on outcome measures see 'Outcomes of Community Care for Users and Carers' (Nocon and Qureshi, 1996).

Having set the idea of outcome measurement in its context there are six ideas presented below which might help measure what really matters to people, incorporate the local experience into the process and involve the front line more effectively than in the past.

1. The experience pathway

The word 'outcome' presents other problems in addition to those above. Use of it buys into a narrow organisational notion of what the purpose of the activity is. It also has a ring of finality which human beings don't experience. Retail chains can rightly celebrate outcomes, the sales which come at the end of their work. But any 'outcome' for a human being is swiftly followed by other outcomes. Life is a series of outcomes and few outcomes are the end of the story. Death is an outcome from which there is no further query, but most of us even under the most hideous pressure, live through things. Even something as traumatic as the removal of a child is not an 'outcome' to the child. The child might remember that event for the rest of her life, but she is as likely to remember what happened in the following days and weeks, experiences that follow the so called 'outcome'. The child will change schools, change placements, go back to her parents. Her life will go on through all these experiences. Human beings 'experience' life in a comprehensive way, possibly paying little attention to the narrow event which for us is an 'outcome'.

Is there merit in trying to capture the service user's reaction to patterns of experience rather than trying to measure their response to artificially identified outcomes? There are many sets of events which contribute to the service user's overall experience that CSSRs, together with partner organisations, help manage. To illustrate the potential of this approach I will describe the path of an older person experiencing a stay in hospital. Think about this and there are a number of events the person will experience; the accident or ill health event, the realisation of the emergency nature of the event, calling an ambulance, an ambulance journey, assessment on arrival at hospital, initial treatment, decision about admission, admission, further assessment and treatment, further assessments, treatment and care planning, assessment for discharge, decision about health care and social care support on discharge, discharge, and the post discharge support arrangements. And this list just captures the organisational view of events, not the feelings of the patient; the fear, the response of relatives, or the practical worries associated with an unplanned stay away from home.

There are a number of organisational outputs and service user 'outcomes' here subject to reporting as PIs. The national PIs covering this pathway are currently managed by four different organisations – the ambulance service, the hospital trust, the PCT, and the CSSR. Yet this experience pathway is about one person. Rather than measuring the so called outcome of each event, if we really wanted to judge how well the whole system is responding to people's needs we should be checking on the total experience of the person on the pathway. Would it be so difficult to get these organisations to share their data and gauge the timeliness and effectiveness of the various events in the system? Would it be so difficult to talk to a sample of the people concerned and check the quality of their whole experience? It would be a real triumph to get the four health and social care players to share data, take each other seriously, judge their mutual effectiveness and investigate blockages together without falling into mutual blame. A lot of effort would be required to set this up – but then four different organisations operate roughly parallel systems anyway. And such an approach would be so much more efficient than the current data duplications. Who knows what operational benefits would follow from sharing this data? Other experience pathways that suggest themselves for this approach include mental health admission hospital stay and discharge, the removal of a child, helping a child move on, assessments for all service user groups, a Child Protection intervention, foster parent assessment, training and the first placement.

2. Let's try different sizes

The phrase 'one size fits all' is often used to decry the big government approach to things. The information panopticon and the central control arrangements have enabled a truly national system of performance measurement. But the system allows no local input. Elements of local priorities could be incorporated into the process to everyone's benefit. To achieve this the activities to be included for measurement and judgement each year could be subject to a formal negotiation within a set of rules. The Key Thresholds would be included automatically in the PI set for all CSSRs and perhaps some other PIs in the PAF set. Each CSSR would, in addition, be expected to suggest the measurement of progress against some local priority initiatives. A principal feature here could be that the CSSR would have to produce evidence from service users that the issue is seen by them as important. Or the CSSR might suggest the measurement of progress against a business process, or the timeliness of a particular response. Again the CSSR would have to provide evidence that the issue is something which concerns staff and whose improvement would benefit service users. An alternative might be to take an idea from the Public Service Agreement and the Local Area Agreement process and ask each CSSR to identify PIs where they have made specific arrangements for improvement. These could, for that year be treated as Key Thresholds, with enhanced status for that CSSR.

This **triangulation** tactic would retain a strong emphasis on **national priorities**, thus allowing benchmarking between authorities and national tracking of key policies. But it would also hook into local need and would be informed by **service users** and **front line staff**. This may be easier for some service user groups than others and it may require some effort, but the potential is there to link national leadership with local concerns and use a nest of objectives triangulated between large outcomes (the government require-ment), individual experiences (the local people's perspective) and practice implementation (the staff contribution). It would also link business planning processes to front line concerns.

This would give impetus to the rather weak requests by the CSCI that CSSRs should develop their own local indicators. But if the CSCI thought that the skills in identifying local data sets and performance measures were too sophisticated it could offer help. The CSCI could play an important role in developing performance templates, briefings and advice and could set up a library of local PIs, much like the AC has. This proposal is more complex than the current process and would require more resources to run it properly. The CSCI would have to ensure that each CSSR measured an acceptably broad range of activities rather than their pet projects. It would also require of the CSCI Business Relationship Managers a more sophisticated understanding of the work of the authority than may currently be the case.

3. A triennial cycle

An adjunct to the previous suggestion is to move away from an annual cycle of judgements. One of the crucial actions taken to support local government in Tony Blair's first term was the move to the three year cycle of financial management and planning. This shifted attention away from the crowded round of local authority finance. So why was an annual approach introduced for performance measurement and assessment? A more sensible strategy would be to operate on a three year cycle, with attention shifting to performance in different parts of the CSSR's activity each year. I can see some problems with this, as three years is a long time for an inspectorate to leave certain activities to fend for themselves, but a real intention to reduce the burden of inspection would incorporate something along these lines.

4. Human qualities

I have argued earlier that in measuring performance quantity and quality are two sides of the same coin. You cannot convince anyone you are providing a decent service unless you demonstrate that you are providing enough of it in a timely manner (quantity) to an acceptable standard (quality). But quantity and quality have fundamentally different attributes. Like the human senses sight and sound they can only be experienced in their own terms and neither tells the whole story. It is possible to watch a play without sound or just to listen to it. But the experience is only complete if you both see and hear it. The quantitative measures which the current performance measurement system relies upon cannot be replaced by qualitative ones, but can be complemented by them. This completion can be achieved in a very obvious way. Take two PAF PIs; PAF AO/C28 *the number of people receiving intensive home care*, and PAF CF/A1 *The number of Looked After Children with more than two placement moves in a year*. For each of them a qualitative element can be easily added to the quantitative report. See the examples below:

Intensive home care

The qualitative element here could be injected into the PI by taking a random selection of those people who have dropped out of the PI over the year reported on; those disabled people who no longer receive 10 hours care. A set of questions discussed with people face to face, after an initial file audit, would seek to find the reasons for dropping out. Some will have died, some will have been admitted to residential care but some will have become more confident or capable of coping in their home so that they need fewer than the 10 hour trigger for the PI. At the same time questions could also be asked about the intrusiveness, quality of care, reliability and so on of the package. The resulting intelligence gained would give a very helpful picture of the impact of the care on the person and check their attitude to their level of independence. To ensure that people did not feel abused by being asked these questions the process could be undertaken as part of the normal review – thus ensuring that any problems could be attended to as a normal part of the work. This would include front line staff in the performance process. Some of these reviews could be undertaken by an independent body to check that 'internal' reviewers did not deliberately paint a rosy picture of the service user experience. The report of these quality reviews would be submitted to the CSCI with the PI. The report would not stand up to statistical scrutiny and it would be important that the temptation to make it do so should be avoided. It is the quality of the experience being sought, not yet another set of statistics. This risks the accusation that what was being reported was mere anecdote. But all individual experience is anecdote. This process proposes to count the activity, as we already do, but to make it more human by adding the anecdotal. It is after all the individual human story which grabs our attention, not the statistic.

Placement moves

The number of children with more than two placement moves in a year is limited even in the biggest council. To get a more complete picture of the meaning of the indicator a file audit could be undertaken of all those with a high number of placement moves. This might look at simple things like age, age match between the child and foster carers, sibling contact, mental health of the child, and so on. The review process could be the vehicle for this investigation. Again this intelligence, collated and reported, links the quantitative report to the front line and child's experience, provides operational intelligence locally and to the CSCI.

This approach could also test the validity of the PI. As for resourcing this approach, if the surveys discussed above were abandoned then the resource directed towards those activities could be redirected to create these 'human quality' aspects to a number of PIs. There is no attempt here to pretend that a qualitative approach could be undertaken for the whole cohort of people caught by these PIs. That would be inordinately expensive and could not be administered in a way that captured human responses which would be useful to CSSRs. Nevertheless some version of this approach could turn the statistical data into management intelligence, test the validity of the PI, test the impact of services on service users, test the impact of the policy and involve front line staff.

5. Using review processes properly

The proposal in the previous sub section relied on the individual case review process for the investigation of the human impact of activity we record for PIs. The purpose of reviews is to identify progress, achievements, threats, drift and so on. All reviews are recorded. Why cannot some use be made of all the data in the records to collate achievements and to judge overall team performance? Effort might be required to record activities in a collatable way. No doubt there needs to be a debate about the ethics of using information collected for one reason for performance measurement purposes. But reviews are universal, and would be relatively easy to harness.

6. Human touchstones

Some of the ideas which underpin the performance measurement framework come from Kaplan and Norton's balanced scorecard. Many local authorities have taken up the idea and balanced scorecards adorn many council web sites. Often these consist of charts occupied by colourful lists of PIs with little discernable connection to each other. And for organisations which are supposed to be citizen focussed the language of the scorecard – inputs, resources, processes, finance and organisational learning – is very formal. Kaplan and Norton's model was devised for commerce and despite its colonisation of the public sector there are questions about whether the balanced scorecard has acclimatised to a more human environment (Speck-bacher, 2003).

The balanced scorecard's purpose is to lay out all the activities which contribute to the organisational outcomes, describe the connections between those activities and plan and manage that activity to make the organisation as effective as possible. It might be better for social care to turn the scorecard on its head and try to identify the detail of the 'outcomes' or experiences we aspire to offer the service user as the starting point – creating a human scorecard rather than an organisational one. This requires an expansion of the focus on the people we are serving and a contraction of the process focus inherent in the traditional balanced scorecard. A starting point for this is to check with people what it is about our services they actually value and develop our understanding of the impact of the results of our activities. This approach is implied by the five outcomes of the 2004 Children Act and the seven outcomes identified for adults by the Green Paper, *Independence, Wellbeing and Choice*. Although helpfully brief and comprehensive the way the outcomes are described has an institutional feel. The outcomes are not couched in the sort of language ordinary people use. So to establish a human scorecard we have to complement these national requirements with what local people say they value.

This exercise has to be done very carefully as ordinary people have the habit of preferring features of our services which surprise professionals. I know one CSSR for instance which completed this exercise for older people, being

ECM	WIC	Included in both
		Improved health
	Improved quality of life	
		Making a positive contribution
Stay safe		
	Exercise choice and control	
	Freedom from discrimination or harassment	
		Economic well being
	Personal dignity	
Enjoy and achieve		

Figure 11 Amalgamated list of desired outcomes for children and adult service users identified in *Independence, Wellbeing and Choice (IWC)* and in *Every Child Matters (ECM)*

especially proud of the choice of menu introduced in one of their services. The people did value this, but much less than other things like having enough to eat and the meals appearing on time. The people in a residential home also took the opposite view to social care managers about the high staff turnover. The residents welcomed this as it meant regular new faces, a tonic in an otherwise repetitive routine. Similarly what people sometimes value about a service is at a tangent to what is offered. In an exercise I conducted recently a group of staff discussing their experience of the hairdresser universally valued the hour or so being pampered more than the rearrangement of their hair. So services will sometimes deliver 'windfall' outcomes. There will also be inadvertent consequences, which people do not appreciate – intrusion in the home, for instance in complex packages of care. But more difficult to respond to is the fact that human beings might value something one day and not the next. So identifying human touchstones has to be a dynamic process.

Set out below is a list as a starting point for discussion. The word touchstone for the aim of our activity is apt. A touchstone is a stone used for testing for gold or silver. The list of touchstones is similar to the list in

---

Human Touchstones
Did they get in touch quickly enough and are they available to me?
Do I understand what they are doing and how they can help?
Do they understand my circumstances and needs?
Do I trust them?
Are they reliable?
Do I feel safe?
Am I in control?
Am I in a better place as a result of what they are doing?

Carer needs
Have I had my say?
Do they understand?
Have I been supported?

Social expectations
Is there a balance between what we do for different family members?
Is there equity of access and provision?
How much do we spend, is it proportionate and does it produce efficient services?
Are our processes efficient, effective and timely?
Do we keep people safe?

Figure 12   Human Touchstones: A starting point for developing a human scorecard for planning and performance management

Independence, Wellbeing and Choice and *Every Child Matters*, but expressed in active language. I have added a societal expectations list which encapsulates the financial and policy requirements which CSSRs have to submit to.

Different organisations, or parts of organisations will identify different touchstones. The touchstones are also dynamic and will change over time so need regular testing with service users. However once touchstones are identified each CSSR is free to work backwards to identify the processes and resources required to match each touchstone. Each touchstone would have sub sets which could be made to cover all the likely points of impact our intervention might have on the person's life. For instance the 'In Control' touchstone might include sub sets and questions, including:

- The proportionality of any intervention.
- The role of parents and other family members in the lives of service users.
- The person's ability to negotiate their own help.
- Our attention to supporting people in risky situations to develop their independence.
- Their financial situation.
- Their ability to manage their own lives.
- Risks.

Once you have identified a series of valued human touchstones the objectives for the organisation becomes easier to identify. It doesn't require the current system to be ripped up, but does demand that we look at the way we identify priorities and what we do about them in a different way.

The final building block on the foundation of touchstones consists of the identification of a number of outcome indicators. We have seen the drawbacks of some types of outcome indicator, so it might be useful to construct an outcome indicator set which uses a range of different approaches. In Figure 13 four distinct types of outcome indicator are identified:

1. Those which check individual service user's **perception** (Outcome Set 1). These will seek comments about several of the identified touchstones, views about whether they feel in control and have good access to services, as well as about satisfaction.
2. Those which test service **effectiveness** (Outcome Set 2). How close does the service get to delivering what is intended?
3. Those which collate the **achievements of (or dangers to) the service user population** compared with the general population (Outcome Set 3). This is a set of social inclusion indicators.
4. Those which gauge the **impact and effectiveness of policy** initiatives (Outcome Set 4).

Individual service user perception

We have seen that asking service users what *they* think has benefits but also drawbacks. Asking people to give their thoughts about a service, their satisfaction about it or the service impact is the only way to get a good response and real intelligence about their circumstances: but skewed, partial or misleading responses must be expected. Two features of **Outcome Set 1** (see Figure 13) differentiate it from the sort of surveys which have been used by the CSCI up to now:

1. Each 'survey' would be carried out as part of the formal review process. This potentially involves a range of front line staff, avoids ethical problems about asking people about difficulties and then doing nothing about it, and gives additional intelligence to the CSSR, as well as measuring the satisfaction, trust, perception etc. of particular aspects of the service. It has the drawback of being administered by the CSSRs themselves: in which case people might not be as honest as they might be with independent 'surveyors'.
2. Each 'survey' would use samples of people already identified as in receipt of a particular type of service, or being in a particular set of circumstances. Thus LAC would be the focus of sets of questions. Those people newly 'helped to live at home', or in receipt of direct payments or those assessed during the previous six months could provide a sample for survey. This has the potential benefit of using the current quantitative PI set as the basis for consideration of outcomes.

In addition to this approach it might be worth considering an addition to the service user data base used by CSSRs to record assessments and care plans. Each of the assessment tools will have some sort of 'service user comments' box or something of that sort. If enquiries were to be made under headed sections with such titles as:

- Overall satisfaction with the service.
- Ease of access to the CSSR.
- Whether treated with dignity or respect.
- Perception of effectiveness of service.

. . . the comments by service users could be recorded, collated at review time and analysed at a later date. The problem here is that it has a tick box feel about it. Nevertheless something like this might be worth considering.

Service impact on the individual

For **Outcome Set 2** the achievement against some specific outcome identified in the care plan is measured, again as part of the review process,

Outcome required	How is outcome success measured	Sample PIs	How is data for PI to be collected?
Outcome Set 1 Feeling in control, ease of access, satisfaction, trust.	Specifically identified SU sample: those subject to assessments, care plans or services over the last year.	No. of people assessed in a given period and receiving a service. What percentage thought access was good, felt part of the process, in control and trusted the service providers? No. of people assessed whose assessment started within two days. What percentage thought the assessment started quickly enough? (another could be, those whose assessment did **not** start within two days).	Data for all these PIs to be collected as part of service review process.
Outcome Set 2 Improved independence, improved or maintained functioning, improved skills.	Specifically identified sample of SU population.	The percentage of people who report that outcomes in the care plan can be achieved (or mostly achieved). (There could be a dual question asking the worker or review panel and service users and carer – thus a dual PI could result, covering different perceptions of the achievements of the plan).	Data for all these PIs to be collected as part of the review process.
Outcome Set 3 Social inclusion achievements and safety.	Socially inclusive achievements of SU population compared with the general population and no. of negative events.	What proportion of SU population has sole access to a car? What percentage of LD SUs under 30 have a mobile phone compared with the general population. GCSE attainment for LAC or access to a PC where they live. No. of cautions or convictions of LAC. Nos. of PD people in 16 hours or more work a week. Percentage of OP SU population with internet access compared to general OP population. No. of falls leading to hospital admission. Percentage of types of service offered to different communities, by ethnic group, age, disability level, gender etc.	Info from general population to be drawn from national or local surveys. Information from SU groups to be administered by annual survey or targeted data collection re negative and positive events.
Outcome Set 4 Success of national social engineering policies.	Measurement of policy achievement.	No. of direct payments received by SUs. No. of adoptions of LAC. No. of Community Care Assessments undertaken in proportion to those approaching LA for help (to reduce the numbers assessed in the light of the policy focus on prevention).	Current collection arrangements and use of the review process.

Figure 13 Outcome sets and PIs

offering the benefits outlined above. This puts a premium on the care planning and review process: concentration on which must strengthen the whole assessment and care planning cycle. The difficulty with this is that outcomes are inevitably individual, and so would be difficult to collate. Also concentration on this approach might lead to care plans being less ambitious than they might be if success against them were not to be formally measured. A few examples however might be helpful:

- A service user to be living in their own home (if this, in the case of an older person, is in jeopardy) at the end of a review period.
- Improved, or maintained attendance at school for a child in need.
- Improved skill level, travelling to a day service on the bus for a person with a learning disability, rather than in supported transport.

Much more individualised and 'smaller' achievements could also be included in a care plan. These achievements are still individual. Crude collation might include whether the primary aims of the care plan have been achieved. Verification is a problem here: staff might report over optimistic improvements to demonstrate good progress. But if one of the overriding aims is to engage front line staff then responsibility must be offered to the front line. The down side of this is that, like a lot of quantitative PIs, collation of such delicate and individual achievements might reduce them to tick boxes.

But there is a great deal of potential here, I think. There may well be merit in investigating ideas from the Soft Outcomes movement or from the Adult Learning RARPA initiative being led by the LSC and NIACE.

Service user population achievement

Outcome Set 3 is relatively easy to derive, and is the approach used currently for PIs with LAC and services offered to people from black and ethnic minority communities. However, the PAF set often uses a proportion, i.e. the closer to '1' the better: using a percentage might be a better approach. Similarly a set of negative events such as falls for older people could be chosen locally from those thought to jeopardise policy goals most.

However care needs to be taken in identifying social inclusion achievements (or excluding events or circumstances) and establishing PIs around such achievements. For people under 30 with a learning disability one of the Social Inclusion Indicators could be individual access to a mobile phone. But this would have to be considered as part of a set of linked indicators, rather than considered individually. If not, a CSSR which wants to score highly could just buy everybody a mobile phone and ignore other aspects of their lives.

Although the most straightforward outcome set this would be potentially the most onerous to deliver for two reasons:

- Annual surveys of the SU population would need to be carried out for many of these PIs, which would require considerable effort.
- Information about the 'achievements' in the general population would need to be available. There are extrapolations about almost anything but local data about the general population's lifestyle and standards would have to be more focussed than extrapolations from national surveys.

Policy impact

Outcome Set 4 is perhaps the most controversial. It posits the establishment of PIs which neither service users nor staff are particularly keen on but might be seen as important in national policy terms. The reduction of residential admissions for older people and replacing that service with a more comprehensive and flexible domiciliary service was the classic example from the 1998 social care priorities. In some places the pressure to make this shift was unpopular with both line managers and staff and was difficult to sell to carers and family members. In addition it also had political difficulties associated with it because the longer term impact of reductions in admissions has seen home closures and business failures. What is more, there was and is no real way of asking service users if they would be more satisfied with a service they have not received, are not aware of and do not understand than that which they have actually received. Other examples include the closure of children's homes, the resettlement from long stay hospitals, the transfer of resources from large day centre facilities to more individual day services for people with learning disability.

A current example from wider local government is about domestic waste. Complicated waste collections involving different bins for different waste materials potentially confuses citizens and frustrates refuse workers. But the policy aim is about increasing recycling, checking the spread of landfill sites, with all the consequences they have, and ultimately contributing to the reduction in global warming. A noble cause few would argue with in the current political climate. So there will be some policy areas where immediate improvements or satisfaction for individual users will not be immediately discernable, but are justifiable nevertheless.

But, of course, such an approach potentially sacrifices the needs of the individual to the greater good: the resort of scoundrel politicians down the ages. So safeguards must be built in. One way to safeguard a service user's rights would be to identify such policy achievements for satisfaction with questions at review time, as in Outcome Set 1. Thus people receiving Direct Payments (a policy imperative) would be formally asked whether they are satisfied. Continued levels of dissatisfaction for those suffering from any policy would alert the CSSR and then the CSCI, DfES and DoH to the questionable nature of the policy. This way both the progress of the policy and the success of it with individuals would be measured at the same time.

Taking it seriously

All the suggestions above require both a shift in thinking and considerable effort. There is no alternative if something valuable is to be made of our performance measurement and assessment system. But attention is also needed to one crucial underpinning feature of the current system, the profile of the process and the potential nfor a more imaginative approach to partnerships.

1. Data quality

Currently it is generally accepted that performance measurement data quality is poor. There are two possible responses to this problem, the stick and the carrot. The National Probation Service (NPS) has gone for the former approach for one aspect of it. When the NPS performance management regime was introduced the culture of reporting performance was undeveloped in probation, and from the beginning there were problems with the timeliness of returns. From 2002 an indicator was established requiring data to be returned by a particular date. This partially worked in that more Probation Areas submitted data on time. But those which did not get the return in on time had no incentive to return data thereafter. This led to data being months late. The following year the NPS introduced a sliding scale of negative consequences for late submission and data timeliness improved.

Of course timeliness is only one feature of data quality. As we have seen there is growing criticism from the centre about the quality of data submitted by CSSRs. But, in my view the DfES, DoH and CSCI only have themselves to blame. Lead in times for the introduction of new measures is too short. Advice, it has been suggested, about the definitions sometimes falls short of clarity. The Autumn 2004 PADI – the analysis tool made freely available in CD form by the CSCI of performance data from all authorities – was inaccurate. As has been noted earlier the staff sent out by the AC to audit BVPIs are often not very knowledgeable and have in the past operated inconsistently. This sloppy attention to data quality is unacceptable. So there are faults at both ends of the spectrum. It is, I think, for the DoH, DfES and CSCI to take the lead in strengthening the partnership between themselves and CSSRs to improve data quality. There are several things that could be done. First of all data quality and data submission standards should be set and introduced – perhaps attracting a PI of their own – developed hand in hand with CSSRs. The CSCI could then operate a yellow card system for CSSRs which do not meet data quality standards and perhaps make a separate judgement each year on the quality, timeliness and audit trail availability of all data submitted. But before any sanctions are levied a comprehensive programme of advice, training, and support should be offered nationally. Current staffing of the CSCI is probably not generous enough to make this sort of partnership a real possibility. Nevertheless something of this sort has to be attempted. The joint AC/CSCI self assessment toolkit on data quality would be a good starting point for discussions about such a programme (Audit Commission, 2005).

2. Profile and partnership

Perhaps too the CSCI should raise the profile of the human element in performance disciplines. The Care Scotland website might show the way forward. This not only includes details of the Performance Improvement Framework, (the Scottish PAF), but includes examples of good practice, related to PIF PIs which have led to real improvements in services. The use of the word 'Improvement' too is interesting. The Scots intend not to use a comparative judgement of CSSRs and instead to concentrate their inspection and performance measurement approach on improvements to service users. This difference between the PAF and the PIF is instructive (see Appendix). For in England the PAF serves the performance assessment process rather than the broader notion of improvement. And CSSRs are not likely to engage singlemindedly with an improvement agenda, while the inspectors' emphasis is still on assessment and judgement.

Another way of taking the process more seriously might be to engage service users in the review and management of the PAF set. Perhaps the CSCI should hand over the design of PIs to service users groups, aided by staff from CSSRs, partner organisations, the LGA and so on. The CSCI could set the broad parameters implicit in the policy imperatives and the minister, of course, would have to agree what was proposed.

Another possibility which would engage staff and managers more effectively might be to draw on the experience of the Research Assessment Exercise (RAE) carried out every few years for higher education bodies (see Appendix). The research excellence rating achieved by each university could not be more important to them – it directly influences their success as businesses and academic institutions. The RAE is not undertaken by 'outsiders' but led by academics. In the 2008 exercise 900 university staff will help conduct this complex peer review exercise. Is there potential to establish peer review amongst CSSRs as the vehicle for judgements about the quality of their services?

And in the end . . .

Of all the thoughts in this chapter the most important is the obligation on managers of CSSRs to establish in the hearts of front line workers a congruent relationship between good practice, good outcomes and good reported performance. Whatever happens to the details of the system it is clear that the government, now it has access to activity and performance data, is unlikely to relinquish its grip on policy direction. It is also unlikely to proceed at anything other than a demanding pace for improvements. But the conundrum identified at the beginning of the chapter has to be confronted if the tensions within the performance assessment system and the resentments caused are not to result in disrepute. The public attitude to 'targets' noted earlier demonstrates that we are not too far away from that. A local dimension and a human element have to be introduced to the process. If achieved CSSRs could respond to the requirement to improve real outcomes for local people and report that reliably. And only then can front line staff play a stronger role in identifying and delivering service improvements.

Exercise

Think about the ideas presented here. Think about other possible ways a human element and local dimension could be incorporated into the current performance measurement processes. Work up those ideas into practical proposals. OK? Now put them into practice.

Appendix: The Other Three Nations and Allied Trades

This book is about the performance measurement and performance assessment processes in social care in the 150 councils with social service responsibilities in England. The other three nations of the UK operate in similar cultural territory, but legislative frameworks and organisational structures are different. The devolutionary arrangements in Scotland, Wales and Northern Ireland introduced during Blair's first administration confirmed existing differences and set the development of social care on varying courses. But the language in social care is familiar across the UK and the general direction set by Whitehall is the same. There are surely lessons each social care economy can draw from the experience of the others.

The three nations

Scotland

There are 32 Scottish Social Work Departments, responsible for social care services for older people, adults, children and offenders. The Scottish Executive introduced in 2005 a Performance Improvement Framework (PIF). This is the broad equivalent of the PAF in England, but encompasses practice elements of performance improvement as well as the quantitative approach adopted by the English PAF. Use of the word Improvement implies an emphasis in Scotland on services rather than assessment of authorities. The PIF complements and partially replaces the existing statutory Performance Indicators reported each year. These have been reported since 1993, after the introduction of the Local Government Act (Scotland) 1992. This was the North British equivalent of John Major's Citizen's Charter legislation. The results of these performance indicators are published annually but contribute to no formal national benchmarking exercise or league tabling. And there has until 2005 been limited relationship between PIs and inspections. The Social Work Inspection Agency, established in May 2005, is tasked with carrying out comprehensive inspections of all 32 Social Work Departments by 2008. These developments replace a somewhat piecemeal approach, similar it seems to the pre 1996 English SSI regime. While there is no legislative equivalent of the English Children Act 2004 the Inspectorate responsible for Education (HMIe) has been working with colleague inspectorates on a programme of inspections of comprehensive public service arrangements for children. There are parallels with the children's Joint Area Reviews in England and many echoes here of the English joint model. Thus the Scottish executive has identified 'seven visions', the equivalent of the English 'five outcomes' for children.

There is an evolutionary feel to these performance measurement arrangements. My impression is that the powers that be in Scotland wish to avoid the more confrontational aspects of the performance assessment arrangements they see in England. The social work community in Scotland is smaller anyway and may be conducive to improvement by peer example, which England, with so many more authorities, may be immune to.

Wales

There are 22 Social Work Departments in Wales, each coterminous with the Local Health Board (LHB) the local health commissioning body, equivalent to the English PCT. Some of these departments are very small. There are Performance Indicators, derived from the Citizen's Charter initiative of the 1990s. That set was confirmed and amended in the Welsh strategy for social services announced in 2001. There is a Social Work Inspectorate (SSIW) which carries out a programme of inspections on the pre 1996 English SSI model. But they are involved in making no comparative judgement about councils or national benchmarking. From 2005 a second round of Joint Reviews started, following the original set completed between 1999 and 2004. These Joint Reviews are a development of the process begun in England in 1996. The judgements made by the SSIW in that first round were tough. No department was found to be 'serving most people well' and only eight were judged to 'have promising prospects'. There seems to be a desire to develop this pattern into something more demanding. The Welsh administration announced in April 2005 a grant aimed at improving the platform for performance measurement, IT databases, staffing and skills.

Northern Ireland

The four Northern Irish Health Boards, have traditionally included a comprehensive social care function. Each Board reports a range of activity and performance against a set of indicators each year and this data is combined into a report, which for 2003/04 was 194 pages long. The data produced is broken down into sub units of each Board and provides precise comparisons between different areas. But you have to wade through the detail for this to become apparent. No formal comparison or judgement is made between the Boards. In such a small community of only four bodies such comparisons would be especially invidious. The Eastern Board, for instance, which includes most of Belfast, would always 'score' worse than, say, the Southern Board made up of smaller and more rural communities.

Northern Ireland has an SSI which undertakes assessments of services as well as regulating individual service provision. The SSI carries out thematic inspections in which inspectors assess and report on a particular aspect of social work or contribution by personal social services and criminal justice agencies. They also carry out 'Total Inspections' in which inspectors assess and report on all of the Board's or Trust's social work services.

My overall impression is that devolution detached Wales and Scotland from the determined pace of performance measurement and assessment in England. Northern Ireland has had long standing separate arrangements. It seems to me that the other three nations are watching England carefully, will pick up aspects of the English system which appeal, but are in no great hurry to copy what they see as the more divisive characteristics.

Public services in England

The pattern of performance measurement and inspection is similar across public service occupations and becoming more uniform. Inspections are giving way to annual assessments, which are becoming interlinked as council 'service block' inspections are being incorporated into the CPA process. 'Service blocks' in CPA terms include housing, adult social care, children's services and so on. Integrated working resulting from the 2004 Children Act and the partnerships developing between health and social care will no doubt lead to shared assessment methodology. There are nevertheless still different flavours to the performance measurement and assessment processes in different public services.

Education

The process adopted for performance measurement and assessment for education has two aspects – the league tables of results and targeted inspections of schools and other educational services. League tables of exam results have been published since 1991 and have been refined to account for 'value added' by the school to the particular mix of deprivation and affluence offered each school by its catchment area. The league tables of results still provoke controversy each year, but less fury than was the case when they were introduced. The inspection process has consisted of:

- The school to be inspected submitting a great deal of data against an Ofsted template. Several months notice have traditionally been afforded the school to be inspected.
- Fieldwork in which several inspectors spend a week in the school observing a range of activities and interviewing staff, students and parents.
- A draft report is prepared containing a judgement about the quality of the school.
- The school has an opportunity to comment about the report before publication.

This familiar pattern was taken up by the AC for the CPA and by the CSCI. Ofsted has announced a development of this. In future (under the framework for inspections of schools operating from September 2005) the school will be asked to submit a self assessment to a lighter template than has previously been the case. The inspection will take place with only days notice and will last only a couple of days. This is a more proportionate approach and requires fewer inspectors. But the 'lighter touch' results in the transfer of a great deal of responsibility for assessment to the school. The short notice is the most telling feature here and will cause considerable unease. But because of the saving in time and effort for the inspectorate it may well herald a move by other inspectorates from the MOT test approach we have become accustomed to, towards something more akin to a Speed Trap (Ofsted, 2005).

Probation

The National Probation Service assessment process is simple and it could be argued, crude. There are a small number of national Performance Indicators, which seem to be precisely related to the work of the service. These are reported regularly and these results and other judgements made by the Inspectorate are combined in what is called a 'weighted scorecard' to produce a precise score for each area. The numerical result places each area in a league table. So each year one NPS area is placed first, one second and so on. For 04/05 Leicestershire and Rutland came first, knocking Dorset off top spot. Cambridgeshire was the most improved area jumping 14 positions, while Hampshire slid 13 points. London and the West Midlands still sit in the relegation zone. The long standing national recording template, the government's determination that the NPS should manage community orders tightly and the measured introduction of IT for front line staff to record their individual activities means that the impact of performance measurement processes on probation staff is clearer and more pressing than in other public services. One result is a level of bitterness amongst some front line staff I have not experienced elsewhere.

There is also a programme of Inspections.

Health

Primary Care Trusts (PCTs) have in the past submitted a Local Delivery Plan on an annual basis. This outlines previous achievements and plans for the coming year. In addition PCTs have reported two sets of performance indicators, Key Performance Indicators, the more important ones, and Balanced Scorecard Indicators. These were grouped in domains as if they contributed to a linked set of activity analysed as if by a balanced scorecard. The Health Care Commission incorporated the reported results against the PIs into an overall judgement expressed as a star rating. For 2005/2006 they are moving away from using a star rating towards a process whereby PCTs are judged against a set of formal standards on a four point scale. The new process is set out in the 2004, *Standards For Better Health*. The new 'Annual Health Check' requires each PCT to complete a self assessment in the spring in which they outline their own perception of progress against 48 standards as red, amber or green. The HCC will validate the assessment over the summer. They will then outline a draft judgement, which after discussion will be made public in the autumn. The stars will go out but the process will be along the same lines – in parallel with social care assessments and the CPA process. The PCTs are the commissioning bodies of the NHS. For hospital trusts, the service providers, the notion of 'Payment by Results' is being introduced. A select set of treatments are recorded precisely and attract specific amounts of funding for each treatment delivered. This replacement for the old block contracting arrangements potentially links finance, activity and performance reporting.

Universities

Universities have to undergo an external review of the quality of the research they undertake. This is called the Research Assessment Exercise (RAE). The RAE assesses the quality of research, enabling higher education funding bodies to distribute public funds for research selectively. Institutions conducting the best research receive a larger proportion of the available grant so that the best quality research is protected and developed across the UK. The RAE takes place every four to five years and the next exercise will be held in 2008. Around £7 billion in research funds will be distributed as a result. The results of the RAE, for each subject, are expressed in a five point scale. These are made public and as a result a pecking order of virtue is established (see http://www.rae.ac.uk/default.htm). The singular feature of the RAE is that it is a peer exercise – run by academics about academics. There is no freestanding 'inspectorate' as there are for other public services. In the 2008 exercise 900 academics have been selected to be panel members in the RAE.

Universities also take great care to advertise their own teaching success, expressed in a range of ways, but mostly in the proportion of 2:1 degrees achieved by their students.

Voluntary Sector

In many ways the voluntary sector has been prepared for tight performance measurement regimes as a result of the commissioning arrangements which have developed since the introduction of the 1990 Community Care Act. NCH for instance has a comprehensive performance management system. Performance Indicators relating to all areas of work operate at national, regional and project level. Standards are set nationally and a quarterly reporting regime allows for comparisons to be made between regions. Annual audits check compliance and audit trails. There will be specific measures related to each funded project as well. In some ways this might appear tighter than the system run by the CSCI. But managers of voluntary organisations may more readily see the benefits of performance measurement because they can introduce their own systems tailored to their own needs. And the focus which performance measurement offers and precise identification of achievements can be used to enhance their reputation with commissioning bodies.

References

Anonymous (2005) Letters. *Community Care*, 16–22 June.

ASCID (2005) *Programme Mandate: Adult Social Care Information Development*. NHS. Health and Social Care Information Centre.

Audit Commission (1992) *Citizens' Charter Indicators: Charting a Course*. London: HMSO.

Audit Commission (1998) *Reviewing Social Services: Guiding You Through*. London: HMSO.

Audit Commission (2000) *On Target: The Practice of Performance Indicators*, June, www.audit-commission.gov.uk/reports/GUIDANCE

Audit Commission (2002) *Performance Breakthrough: Improving Performance in the Public Sector*.

Audit Commission (2005a) *Service Assessment Frameworks: A Consultation Supporting Comprehensive Performance Assessment for Single Tier and County Councils From 2005 to 2008*. London: Audit Commission.

Audit Commission (2005b) *Social Services Performance Assessment Framework (PAF) Data Quality Audit., 2004/2005*, 31/3/2005. Available at www.audit-commission.gov.uk/subject.asp?

Audit Commission (2005c) *The Harder Test*. Available at www.audit-commission.gov.uk/CPA/Downloads/Oct05CPATheHarderTest.pdf

Audit Commission and CSCI (2005) *Promoting Data Quality in Social Services Performance Information: A Self Assessment Tool for Councils with Social Services Responsibilities*. www.csci.org.uk

Ball, R. and Monaghan, C. (1993) Performance Review: Threats and Opportunities. *Public Policy and Administration*. 8: 3, 33–45.

Beresford, P. (2005) Conference Report. *Community Care*. 26th May to 1st June.

Blair, A. Comment made on 6th July 1999, see http://news.bbc.co.uk/1/hi/uk_politics/3750847.stm

Blalock, A.B. (1999) Evaluation Research and the Performance Management Movement: From Estrangement to Useful Integration? *Evaluation*. 5: 2, 117–49.

Bourne, M. et al. (2000) Designing, Implementing and Updating Performance Measurement Systems. *International Journal of Operations and Production Management*. 20: 7, 754–71.

Bourne, M. et al. (2003) Why Some Performance Measurement Initiatives Fail; Lessons From the Change Management Literature. *International Journal of Business Performance Management.* 5: 2, 245–69.

Cabinet Office Efficiency Unit (1988) *Improving Management in Government: The Next Steps.* London: HMSO.

Carter, N. (1989) Performance Indicators; 'backseat driving' or 'hands off' control? *Policy and Politics.* 17: 2, 131–8.

CSCI (2005a) *Social Services Performance Assessment Framework Indicators 2004–2005.* Nov www.csci.org.uk/council_performance/paf

CSCI (2005b) *Performance Assessment of Social Care Services: Operating Policies 2005.* www.csci.org.uk/council

Davies, M. (1981) *The Essential Social Worker.* Ashgate Publishing.

De Waal, A.A. (2003) Behavioural Factors Important for the Successful Implementation and use of Performance Management Systems. *Management Decision.* 41: 8, 688–97.

Dixon. J. (2005) Green Paper Comment. *Community Care.* June 16–22.

DoH (1990) *The Children Act 1989; Guidance and Regulations Volume One.* London: HMSO.

DoH (1998) *Modernising Social Services.* www.dh.gov.uk/PublicationsAnd Statistics or www.archive.official-documents.co.uk/document/cm41/4169/4169.htm

DoH (1999) *Modernising Health and Social Services: National Priorities Guidance 2000/01–2002/03.* www.dh.gov.uk/PublicationsAndStatistics/Publications/PublicationsPolicyAndGuidance/PublicationsPolicyAndGuidanceArticle/fs/

DoH (2005) *Independence, Wellbeing and Choice.* Green Paper. London: HMSO.

Froggatt, L. (2002) *Love, Hate and Welfare.* The Policy Press.

Guardian Society (2004) Striking Differences. *The Guardian Society.* 24/11/04.

Hunter, A. (2005) Conference Report. *Community Care.* 26 May–1 June.

Improvement and Development Agency (IDeA) www.idea-knowledge.gov.uk/idk/core/page.do?

Improvement and Development Agency (undated) *Making Performance Management Work: A Practical Guide.* www.idea.gov.uk

Improvement Development Agency (2005) Interim findings from research into performance management in well-performing local authorities. www.idea-knowledge.gov.uk/idk/aio/634935

Independence, Wellbeing and Choice (Green Paper) 32, 64, 110, 112

Kaplan, R. (2000) Overcoming Barriers to Balanced Scorecard Use in the Public Sector. *Harvard Business School Press.* Nov/Dec. 10–1.

Kaplan, R. and Norton, D. (1992) The Balanced Scorecard: Measures that drive Performance. *Harvard Business Review.* Jan/Feb.

Ladyman, S. (2005) Independence Equals Dignity. *The Guardian*. 02/03/05.

Lawton. A. and Rose. A. (1994) *Organisation and Management in the Public Sector.* Pitman Publishing.

Lingle. J. and Schiemann. W.A. (1996) From Balanced Scorecard to Effective Gauges: is Measurement Worth it? *Management Review*. 85: 56–61.

Local Government Association (undated) *Performance Management*. lga.gov.uk

Locke, E. and Latham, G.P. (1990) *A Theory of Goal Setting and Task Performance.* Englewood Cliffs, NJ: Prentice Hall.

London Borough of Hillingdon (1999) *Social Services Information Strategy.* http://www.hillingdon.gov.uk/social/strategies/ss_strategy_1999.pdf

Maddock, S. (2002) Making Modernisation Work: New Narratives, Change Strategies and People Management in the Public Sector. *The International Journal of Public Sector Management*. 15: 1, 13–43.

Miller. N. (2004) *Performance Assessment Framework (PAF) Performance Indicators: Guidance and Critical Appraisal, Vol. 1.* Adult Services Social Service Research Group. www.ssrg.org.uk

Nocon, A. and Qureshi, H. (1996) *Outcomes of Community Care for Users and Carers.* Open University Press.

ODPM (1998) *Modern Local Government: In Touch with the People.* www.odpm.gov.uk/stellent/groups

ODPM (2001) *Strong Local leadership, Quality Public Services.* http://www.odpm.gov.uk/stellent/groups/odpm_control/documents/contentser vertemplate/odpm

ODPM (2002) *The National Strategy for Local e-Government.* www.localegov.gov.uk/

ODPM (2004) *Best Value Performance Indicators, General Survey 2003/2004.* June. Topline report.

Ofsted (2005) *Every Child Matters: Framework for the Inspection of Schools in England from September 2005.* www.ofsted.gov.uk/publications/index

Osborne, D. and Gaebler, T. (1992) *Reinventing Government: How the Entrepreneurial Spirit is Transforming the Public Sector.* Addison-Wesley.

Pearce, J. and King, A. (2004) *Performance Assessment Framework: Commentary on Performance Indicators. Vol. 2; Children's Indicators 2002/2003.* 4th edn, Social Services Research Group. www.ssrg.org.uk

Pinkney, S. (1998) The Reshaping of Social Work and Social Care. in Hughes, G., and Lewis, G. (Eds.) *Unsettling Welfare.* Routledge.

Qureshi, H. (2000) Summarising Intended Outcomes For Older People at Assessment. in Qureshi, H. et al. *Outcomes in Social Care Practice.* SPRU, University of York.

Qureshi, H. (2002) Outcomes and Assessment with Older People. *The Research Findings Register.* Summary number 750. http://www.ReFeR.nhs.uk/ViewRecord.asp?ID=750

Raine, J.W. and Willson, J. (1997) From Performance Measurement to Performance Enhancement: An Information System Case-Study from the Administration of Justice. *Public Money and Management.* Jan–Mar, 19–25.

Ramsey, P. (2001) Designing and Implementing Performance Management of Social Care Block Contracts in Fareham/Gosport Social Services Locality. *Managing Community Care.* 9: 2, 41–8.

Rho Delta Quality Solutions in Community Services (1997) *Joint Reviews: What, Why, How? A report of the Rho Delta Seminars on Joint Reviews.* London: Rho Delta.

Rigby. D. (2001) Management Tools and Techniques: A Survey. *California Management Review.* 43: 2, 139–60.

Rodrigues, J. (1992) Curtain up on Performance. *Local Government Chronicle.* 20, Nov.

Samuel. M. (2005) The Personal Touch. *Community Care.* April 14–20, 28–30.

Smith, P. (1993) Outcome Related Performance Indicators and Organisational Control in the Public Sector. *British Journal of Management.* 4: 135–51.

Speckbacher, G. (2003) The Economics of Performance Management in Non Profit Organisations. *Non Profit Management and Leadership.* 13: 3, 267–81.

Stewart, J. (2000) *The Shape of British Local Government.* Macmillan.

Sutch, Dom. A. Quoted on *Thought for the Day* on BBC Radio 4's *The Today Programme* on 17/3/05.

The Children Act 1989; Guidance and Regulations, 1990.

Trafford Metropolitan Borough. *Speakeasy Project.* www.trafford.gov.uk/news/issues/55/articles_speakeasy_project.asp

Unattributed (1989) Ridley Roughs up Quality Plans. *Local Government Chronicle.* 14 April.

Walters, M. (Ed.) (1995) *The Performance Management Handbook.* London: Institute of Personnel and Development.

Wells et al. (2001) Selecting Outcome Measures for Child Welfare Settings: Lessons for Use in Performance Management. *Children and Youth Services Review.* 23: 2, 169–99.

West Midlands ADSS Performance Network (2004) *Making it Real.* www.secta.co.uk

Yerkes, R.M. and Dodson, J.D. (1908) The Relation of Strength of Stimulus to Rapidity of Habit-Formation. *Journal of Comparative Neurology and Psychology.* 18, 459–82.

Glossary

Annual Performance Assessment (APA)   Annual self assessment required by CSCI, Ofsted and DfES from all councils about all the services they offer children and families. This forms the basis of the annual evaluation of performance.

Annual Review Meeting (ARM)   Annual (summertime) meeting between each CSSR senior management and CSCI representative to discuss the performance in the previous year. The CSCI then send an Annual Review Letter to the CSCI outlining their view of the CSSR's performance. This is now only for services for adults and older people. The contents of this letter in 2005 were referred to as the Record of Performance Assessment (ROPA).

Audit Commission (AC)   Government body responsible for auditing and inspection of public services.

Audit Commission Performance Indicators (ACPIs)   A set of performance indicators introduced in 1993 that councils were obliged to collect and report on annually. They were replaced by BVPIs in 1999.

Best Value   Regime introduced by the ODPM in 1998 requiring each council to fundamentally review all services against quality and cost standards following a particular review format. The regime also required annual reporting of achievements and planned improvements. The CPA process, with its more rigorous external investigation of services, has replaced the review element of Best Value. The language of 'continuous improvement' and 'step changes' remains.

Best Value Performance Indicator (BVPI)   Selection of performance indicators (some from the PAF set) flagged as BVPIs. These are subject to formal external audit and are actively considered in the CPA process.

Commission for Social Care Inspection (CSCI)   Independent body responsible for regulating and inspecting social care service provision and the overall performance of councils with social services responsibilities. The CSCI replaced the SSI (which had inspected and assessed local authority social care services as a whole) and the National Care Standards Commission (which registered and inspected individual service providers, both public and private). According to the CSCI itself, the acronym should be pronounced as the letters indicate, never as 'Csky'. The issue here is that the Social Care Institute for Excellence, (www.scie.org.uk/) is known as 'sky'. Saying 'Csky' meaning the CSCI is seen as too confusing.

Corporate Performance Assessment (CPA)   Assessment process led by the AC which results in an overall judgement of the performance of the whole of each council's services.

Council with Social Services Responsibilities (CSSR)   Phrase used by government agencies to describe councils with social service responsibilities. This was in response to the various amalgamations between various council departments resulting in the disappearance of the use of the title social service department from many councils.

Delivery and Improvement Statement (DIS)   Annual Statement of achievements, plans, risks and contingencies submitted to the CSCI by each CSSR about social care services for adults and older people. The DIS also requires CSSRs to report their performance against a range of performance indicators.

Department for Education and Science (DfES)   Government department overseeing, among other things social care services for children.

Department of Health (DoH)   Government department overseeing the NHS and social care for adults and older people.

Improvement and Development Agency (IDeA)   Government funded management development body for local government.

Joint Area Review (JAR)   Comprehensive inspection of all public services for children and families on a three year cycle involving several different inspection bodies.

Joint Review   Now defunct comprehensive inspection of social services departments led jointly by the AC and SSI. Joint Reviews are still used in Wales.

Key Performance Indicators (KPIs)   Loosely used phrase describing the most important indicators in a set of Performance Indicators

Key Thresholds (KTs)   Selection of PIs from the PAF set for which the CSCI sets performance thresholds. If CSSRs do not reach the various threshold performance they are debarred from being judged as serving 'some' (or in some cases 'most') people well. This restricts the Star Rating the CSSR can achieve. These are the most important PIs in the PAF set.

Learning and Skills Council (LSC)   Body responsible for funding and planning all non-university education and training for over 16 year olds in England.

Local Government Association (LGA)   Body representing the interests of all local government bodies.

Local Public Service Agreement (LPSA)   Agreement between local authority and a government department that the council will achieve agreed objectives over a number of years in exchange for a set amount of prize money.

Looked After Children (LAC)   Child in the care of the local authority

National Institute of Adult Continuing Education (NIACE)   NGO set up to promote the study and general advancement of adult continuing education in England and Wales.

Office of the Deputy Prime Minister (ODPM)   Government department responsible for local government. The ODPM drives the development of the Corporate Performance Assessment, as such driving the emerging pattern of performance assessment across the whole of public service. In New Labour's first term the department was called the Department of Environment, Transport and the Regions (DETR). Then it became the Department of Local Government Transport and the regions (DLTR). In 2002 it became the ODPM.

Office of Standards in Education (Ofsted) The inspection body for schools and other primary and secondary education functions. Ofsted works closely with the CSCI on the integrated assessment of local authority children's services. Set to take over the inspection functions for all public services for children in 2008.

Performance Management See the beginning of Chapter 3 for full discussion.

Performance Indicator (PI) A quantifiable measurement of an activity, agreed in advance, which reflects a critical success factor of an organisation.

Performance Measure Organisational activity chosen to represent the success of the organisation. A performance measure in retail industry would be the number of sales achieved. Often used interchangeably with PI.

Performance Measurement The process of measuring success across an organisation's objectives.

Performance Assessment This phrase is used here to mean the process of assessing overall performance of a CSSR by external inspection bodies such as the CSCI and Ofsted.

Performance Assessment Framework (PAF) Framework of 50 performance indicators each CSSR has to report progress against annually which are formally considered as part of the evidence for the annual performance assessment.

Public Service Agreement (PSA) Agreement between government departments that particular policy objectives will be reached within a certain period of time. These agreements are usually between service departments and the Treasury – the PSA being set in return for additional funding.

Quality Protects (QP) Regime of grants, objectives and formal reporting introduced in 1998 to revitalise local authority children's services. QP processes are now incorporated in mainstream funding and expectations.

Referrals, Assessments and Packages of Care (RAP) Data set devised by the DoH covering adults and older people service activities. RAP became fully operational in 2000 when CSSRs were required to report considerable new data about their service activities.

Social Services Inspectorate (SSI) Now defunct inspectorate of social service departments. SSI managers were instrumental in setting up the PAF and Star Rating system. Northern Ireland, Scotland and Wales still have SSIs.

Star Rating Soon to be replaced rating of CSSRs against national standards and criteria. Each CSCR is judged on a four point scale incorporating judgements about how well it is serving people and what its prospects are for improvement.

Index